CW01338604

AFRICAN VIOLETS

BACK TO THE BASICS
Your Questions Answered

by

MELVIN J. ROBEY

Author of:

African Violets: Queens of the Indoor Gardening Kingdom
And
African Violets: Gifts from Nature

Bloomington, IN   authorHOUSE®   Milton Keynes, UK

AuthorHouse™
1663 Liberty Drive, Suite 200
Bloomington, IN 47403
www.authorhouse.com
Phone: 1-800-839-8640

AuthorHouse™ *UK Ltd.*
500 Avebury Boulevard
Central Milton Keynes, MK9 2BE
www.authorhouse.co.uk
Phone: 08001974150

© 2006 Melvin J. Robey. All rights reserved.

No part of this book may be reproduced, stored in a retrieval system, or transmitted by any means without the written permission of the author.

First published by AuthorHouse 12/11/2006

ISBN: 978-1-4259-6201-2 (sc)
ISBN: 978-1-4259-6210-4 (hc)

Printed in the United States of America
Bloomington, Indiana

This book is printed on acid-free paper.

'Norseman'   Courtesy of the African Violet Society of America

OTHER BOOKS BY THE AUTHOR

Home Lawn Care

Lawns:
The year-round lawn care handbook for all climates and conditions, plus a special section on ground covers.

African Violets: Queens of the Indoor Gardening Kingdom

African Violets: Gifts from Nature

Golf History
Unusual facts, figures, and little known trivia
Book One from 1400-1960

FUTURE BOOKS TO BE PUBLISHED BY AUTHOR

African Violet Series
African Violets: Gifts from Nature
to be reprinted as a series of three books,
with new material included

Golf History
Unusual facts, figures, and little known trivia
Book Two from 1960 to 2000

Outdoor Gardening Made Easy

Death Lurks In The Garden

For information on any of these books contact the author at
Mrobey@dc.rr.com

Please turn this page for a review of new books →

GOLF HISTORY

Unusual facts, figures, & little known trivia
by
Melvin J. Robey

While browsing through the pages of this paperback book you will find yourself following in the footsteps of those who walked down the fairways ahead of you into golf history. During your fascinating journey you will discover a collection of golf memorabilia, bizarre incidences, little known tidbits plus an array of golf folklore.

- Which U.S. Presidents names are closely associated with the Walker Cup?
- What does a penny pack of garden seeds and the Ryder Cup have in common?
- Fore. Mulligan. Bogey. Caddie. 19th Hole. What is the origin of these commonly used golf terms?
- What two famous celebrities were caught playing golf at an exclusive country club in their undershorts?
- Why did an indignant Scottish gentleman tell Sam Snead, "My God sir! That's St. Andrews"?

Special offer for African violet enthusiasts with golfers in their family

USA/Canada
$9^{25} + P&H $1^{50} (This is a limited offer and may be cancelled at anytime)

To learn more about the book, the author, and for a brief preview of *Golf History* visit: www.1stbooks.com/bookview/9259 or contact the author at: Mrobey@dc.rr.com.

Send check or money order to:
M.J. Robey
4979 W. Mountain Hill Drive
West Jordan, Utah 84084

THE PERFECT GIFT FOR THE GOLFER IN YOUR FAMILY

AFRICAN VIOLETS: Gifts from Nature
THE SERIES

Mel Robey's second book, *African Violets: Gifts from Nature* was called "Truly a Masterpiece." This original classic is out of print and has become a collector's item. Due to the enthusiastic interest in this book it will soon be back in print. The author has made arrangements for the information to be released in three separate books, the contents of each book are shown below. New information will be added to each one.

Whether your goal is to enjoy beautiful African violets for display in your home, to become an expert grower of these lovely plants, or to develop a deeper understanding of how these plants function, this series of books is adapted to meet your interests.

BOOK ONE
CH 1   African Violets: Everyone's Bloomin' Favorite
CH 2   History of African Violets at a Glance
CH 3   Why Your African Violets Won't Flower
CH 4   Botany of the African Violet Plant
CH 5   Portrait of the Gesneriaceae Family
Glossary

BOOK TWO
CH 6   Understanding Your Potting Mixture
CH 7   Pots and Your African Violets
CH 8   African Violet Plant Food
CH 9   Water and the Plant
CH 10   Environmental Factors Influence Growth of AVS
CH 11   Light: Its Role in the African Violet Kingdom

BOOK THREE
Death of a Five Year Old
CH 13   Pesticides: Are They Safe?
CH 14   African Violet Pests
CH 12   Propagation of African Violets
CH 15   Seeds; A Fascinating Way to Grow African Violets
CH 16   The ABC's of Hybridization

Check the *African Violet Magazine* for information on when these books will be available. Also, go to www.authorhouse.com/bookstore and type in the author's name. Or contact the author at: Mrobey@dc.rr.com

TABLE OF CONTENTS

Chapter 1	INTRODUCTION	1
Chapter 2 Q. 1 - 44	GETTING TO KNOW YOUR PLANTS	4
Chapter 3 Q. 45 - 73	PLANT FOOD ESSENTIAL FOR HEALTHY PLANTS	20
Chapter 4 Q. 74 - 101	POTTING MIXTURES:KEY TO BEING SUCCESSFUL	30
Chapter 5 Q. 102 - 105	CONTAINERS FOR GROWING BEAUTIFUL AFRICAN VIOLETS	42
Chapter 6 Q. 124 - 151	PROPER WATERING TECHNIQUES IMPORTANT	51
Chapter 7 Q 152 - 178	THOSE UGLY PESTS Insects, Diseases, & Other Unsightly Problems	62
Chapter 8 Q. 179 - 208	PROPAGATION IS EASY	72
Chapter 9 Q. 108 - 230	THE ENVIRONMENT AROUND OUR PLANTS	83
Chapter 10 Q. 231 - 250	LIGHT AND ITS ROLE IN A PLANT'S LIFE	91
GLOSSARY		99

CHAPTER 1

INTRODUCTION

Since my first book, *African Violets: Queens of the Indoor Gardening Kingdom*, was published in 1980 I have discovered these lovely plants wherever I have traveled. Fortunately I have been able to visit numerous countries in this quest. If you have a copy of my second book, *African Violets: Gifts from Nature*, three of the color photographs were a result of a trip to England.

It took me two trips to the British Library in London to obtain one of the color photographs. It was the original botanical illustration of the African violet (used as the cover picture for my first book), published in 1895 in the *Curtis Botanical Magazine*. I finally found it fifteen minutes before the library closed. The next problem I faced was I had scheduled an early morning flight home the following day. This meant I could not return the next day to arrange to have a copy of the photograph made for me.

One of the librarians listened to my sad tale and with the typical British sense of humor told me "Cheerio mate." Fortunately for me he was only joking. He suggested I leave my address with him plus a twenty pound bill, assuring me he would personally make sure I received the photograph. Two weeks later it arrived—with change.

On another trip to London I had the opportunity to visit the annual Chelsea Flower Show. This is the most impressive flower show I have seen in my travels and well worth your time if you have an opportunity to spend a day there. The Belgium Embassy exhibit especially caught my attention when I noticed they were using African violets as a border planting. The purple, pink, and white flower combinations were absolutely stunning. The House of Rochford's, a garden nursery, had used African violets for a massive show of color in another location at the Chelsea Flower Show. It was a brilliant display of the plant's dazzling beauty.

When I was working on my second book, *African Violets: Gifts from Nature*, I decided I wanted to do the photography. This required two things, a new 35mm camera with a close-up lens and over 5,000 plants in my home. The few visitors I allowed into my plant room were not impressed with the condition or appearance of all my plants, but they were certainly overwhelmed by the number (as I often was when it was time to water them). To obtain the types of photographs I needed for the book I had to have beautiful plants as well as many, many more showing various diseases, growth problems, propagating techniques, growing practices, and seedling development.

In deciding to write a third book on African violets I elected to use a different approach. Over the years I have been asked numerous questions on various aspects of growing African violets. As a result I chose to present the information in the question and answer format. One of the advantages to this approach is it provides the reader with a quick way to discover the solution to any problem they may be having with their plants.

FIRST TO SEE AN AFRICAN VIOLET

Who was the first person, of non-African ancestry, to gaze upon the pretty little purple flowering plants? A good case can be made for the honor to go to Dr. David Livingstone. In the late 1800's Dr. Livingstone was in search of the source of the Nile River in Africa. His journey took him through the heart of the area where the first African violet seeds were collected. If Livingstone was the first, then the second place honor has to be given to Henry Morgan Stanley.

It was at the end of Stanley's eighth month trek across Tanzania in 1881 searching for Dr. Livingstone that Stanley made his famous greeting, "Dr. Livingstone, I presume?" And perhaps his second comment was, "Did you happen to notice all those unusual plants with those beautiful purple flowers?" If he did make this comment about the African violets, his first comment upon finding Dr. Livingstone has long overshadowed it.

Stanley's journey, as near as I have been able to determine, took him north of Mt. Tongwe and then between the Nguru and Usambara Mountains. Mt. Kilimanjaro would also have dominated much of the skyline during this time. Since Stanley was a naturalist it is easy to speculate he noticed several of the *Saintpaulia* species during his journey. The ones he most likely saw were: *S. confusa, S. magungensis, S. orbicularis, S. shumensis, S. tongwensis,* and *S. veltina*. It is also easy to speculate he never saw *S. ionantha* since his journey started approximately two hundred miles south of the city Tanga, where this species was discovered in 1892.

African Violets Back to the Basics

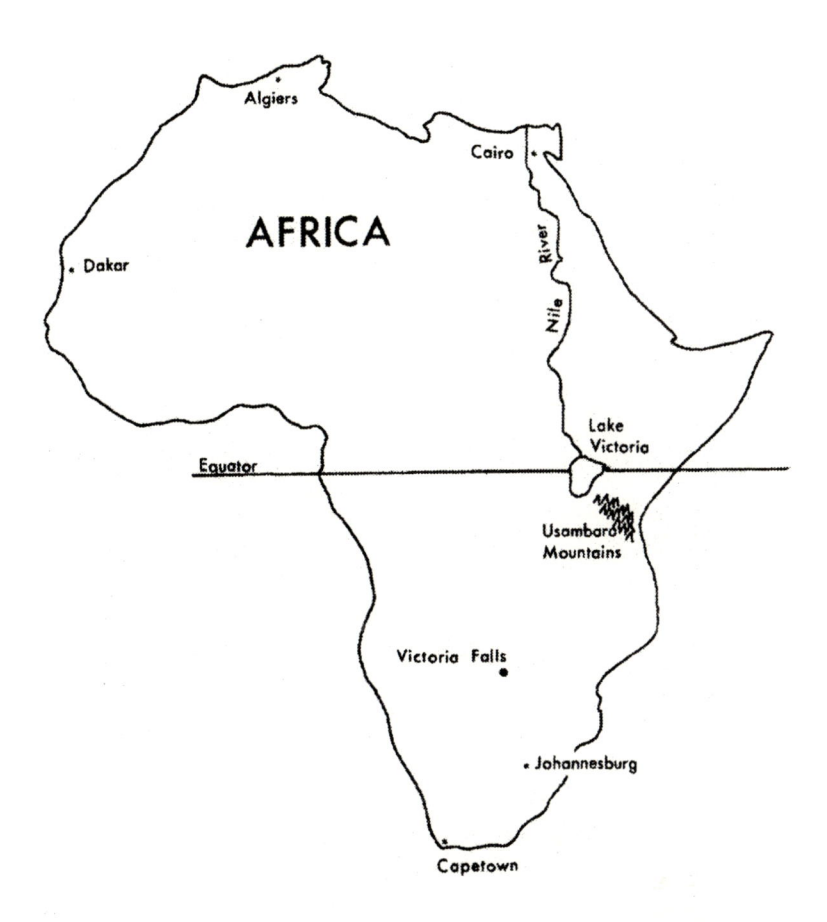

Baron Walter von Saint Paul discovered African violets growing wild in the Usambara Mountains in Tanzania. From *African Violets: Queens of the Indoor Gardening Kingdom*.

CHAPTER 2

GETTING TO KNOW YOUR PLANTS

Question 1 **Could you make a list of the features that make African Violets the Number One flowering houseplant in the world?**

Compiling a list of why African violets are such a popular flowering houseplant is an easy task. I have arranged them in the order that has infatuated me with African violets. I am certain other African violet fanciers would arrange this list differently and could add to it since each individual looks for something different in their plants.

Here is my list:
- Growing African violets is not a difficult task to master
- Excellent support when you are a member of the African Violet Society of American; the bi-monthly *African Violet Magazine* offers members a continuous source of information
- Ease with which the plants can be propagated from leaf cuttings has done much to keep African violets popular in gardening circles around the world
- Ability to produce flowers year round has a tremendous influence on the popularity of African violets
- Gorgeous flowers of all shapes and colors
- The overall appearance of the plant is attractive and adds a nice touch of elegance to any room in which they are being grown
- A wide selection in attractive leaves makes the plants very interesting
- Receiving praise from friends for being able to grow such beautiful flowering plants
- Due to the small size of the plants very little space is needed in the home for growing these lovely plants

- The annual AVSA Convention provides and opportunity to meet other enthusiasts and to make new friends

Question 2   **I am interested in joining a club which will help me in my new hobby of growing African violets. Are there any clubs devoted especially to these lovely plants?**

Yes. There are two excellent organizations you may wish to join. Both publish magazines full of helpful information on African violets. The following information will allow you to contact them.

African Violet Society	American Gloxinia and
of America	Gesneriad Society
2375 North Street	15105 South Seminole Drive
Beaumont, Texas 77702	Olathe, Kansas 66062-3004
Web Site: www.avsa.org	Web site: www.aggs.org

Question 3   **Who discovered the African violet plant?**

Baron Walter von Saint Paul, the governor of German East Africa in the late 1800's is credited with being the discoverer of the African violet. In 1892 he collected seed from the tiny purple flowering plants and sent them to the Director of the Royal Botanical Gardens in Germany.

The first article describing the African violet was written in 1893 by Hermann Wendland and published in the horticultural journal *Gartenflora*. In 1895 the *Curtis Botanical Magazine* described the African violet and provided the world with the first detail drawings of the plant and its flowers.

From this beginning, the African violet has become the favorite indoor flowering plant of the world—Queen of the Indoor Gardening Kingdom!

Question 4   **How many different types of plants are in the Gesneriaceae Family?**

There are 2,000 species in the Gesneriaceae family and they are divided into 120 genera. Of all of these plant types approximately 250 to 300 have been found growing in gardens or containers. Some of the more common ones being: African violets, gloxinia, *Columnea, Episcias, Streptocarpus, Achimenes,* and *Aeschynanthus*.

Question 5   **Gesneriaceae is a funny name for a plant. From where did it originate?**

If Mr. von Gesner were alive today he probably would not appreciate your saying he had a funny name. Konrad von Gesner (1516-1565) of Zurich, Switzerland was a well-known plant collector and taxonomist (person who names and classifies plants). He gave his namesake to the family when he discovered several related plants had not been categorized into a botanical family. Some of the more familiar plants in this family are: African violets, *Sinningia* (florist gloxinia), *Episcias*, and *Achimenes*.

Courtesy of the African Violet Society of America

Question 6 African violets were first discovered growing in African but do these plants grow naturally anywhere else in the world?

No. However, other members of this family of plants may be found growing in a variety of habitats throughout the world.

Achimenes	Jamaica
Boea	Australia, East Indies, and Malaysia
Columnea	South America
Episcia	Mexico and Brazil
Streptocarpus	Africa and Madagascar
Sinningia (florist gloxinia)	Brazil to Mexico

Question 7   **Are African violets and the common garden violet related?**

I would have to answer this question by saying yes, and then qualify the answer. These two flowering plants are related only in the sense they are both in the same natural order of life—the Plant Kingdom. Beyond this they have little in common and are found in entirely different plant families. African violets belong to the Gesneriaceae Family and true violets to the Violiaceae Family. No real close ties whatsoever exist between these two distinct plant families.

Question 8   **The fragrance of many plants when in bloom is such a pleasant one. Are there any African violet species or varieties that have fragrant blossoms?**

To my knowledge there is not a single member in the *Saintpaulia* genus that has fragrant blossoms. It is too bad because with year round flowering the aroma of a blossoming plant would be welcome in almost every home. It does not look like there is much of a chance of any future hybrid African violets having fragrance.

BOTANY OF THE AFRICAN VIOLET PLANT

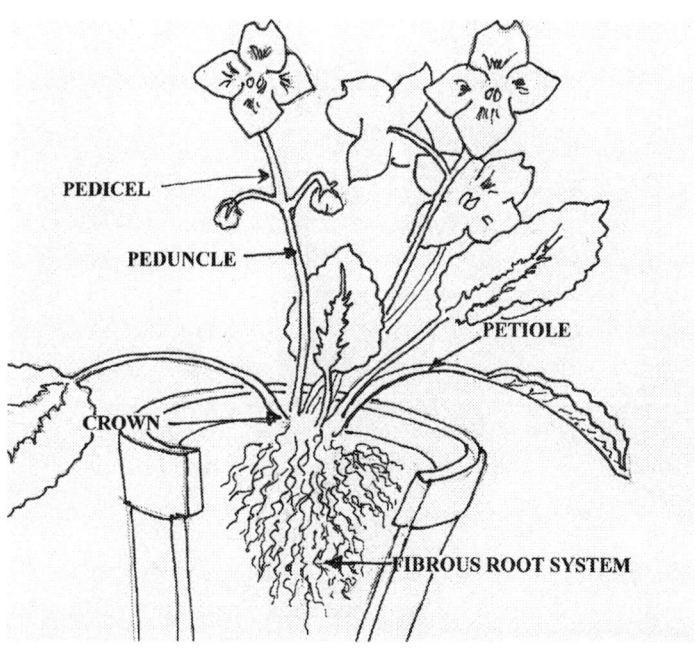

Each part of an African violet plant has a special botanical name for identification.

Question 9 **Can you explain the differences between the terms genus and species?**

First of all you need to know all plants are given a scientific name, which consists of two parts. The first part being called the genus, and the last part is known as the species.

A common genus name is given to all plants having similar flower and fruit characteristics. A genus name may denote the geographic area where the plants were discovered or be named after the person who found them. For example the genus name for the African violet was chosen to honor Baron von St. Paul who introduced the flowering plants to the world outside of Africa.

The species designation is usually a descriptive term highlighting an interesting feature of the plant, for example: *grandifolia*—having large leaves and *diplotricha*—two types of hairs on a single leaf.

<u>African Violet Scientific Name</u>
Saintpaulia   *ionantha*
(genus)   (species)

All scientific names, when typed should be italicized and when hand written they should be underlined.

Question 10 **Will there ever be an African violet with vibrant yellow blossoms?**

I believe one day you will be able to buy African violets with beautiful vibrant yellow blossoms. For years everyone thought a yellow blossom was not a possibility and then a mutant (sport) was discovered with traces of yellow pigments in the petals. Since then hybridizers have been getting closer to developing a blossom with a strong yellow color. In correspondence with Dr. Jeff Smith, columnist for the *African Violet Magazine* and renowned for his genetic studies of the African violet, about the possibility of having a yellow blossom I received the following information: [hybridizers} "...are pretty close to [developing] full yellow flowers. The amount of yellow is still variable and the flowers don't last as long as other colors, but sometimes the flowers are a pure buttercup yellow."

Question 11 **Is it safe to assume the African violets I buy from the local greenhouse dealers and mass merchandisers are free from bugs and diseases?**

Never take any plant into your home and immediately place it with the rest of your plants. Always put the new plant through a quarantine period to ensure there are no hidden problems with the plant. Never assume it is insect or disease free, whether a plant comes from a reputable greenhouse dealer, a commercial grower of African violets, or a close friend.

UNDERSTANDING YOUR PLANTS

Question 12 **Everyone I talk to about my African violets tells me a different way of caring for my plants. How can I be successful growing African violets when I cannot find two "experts" who will agree on the daily needs of African violet plants?**

Do not worry about all the different answers you get from other African violet hobbyists. Each grower started out with varying degrees of knowledge on the basic needs of their plants. Over the years they have done some experimenting, changing the rules to fit their individual needs. African violets have a terrific ability to adapt to their particular owners growing techniques and this is one of the primary reasons these plants are so popular.

Study the basic needs of an African violet as discussed in this chapter and elsewhere. After you are confident in your knowledge of what you are doing start testing your own ideas. It will not be long before your African violets are as beautiful as those of the other "experts" and you will find yourself well on the way to joining the ranks of the Master growers of African violet.

Question 13 **What should I look for when I am selecting an African violet at the garden center?**

First, the plant's overall health and appearance has to be a standout feature. Do not buy a sick plant, even at a bargain, thinking you can improve its condition. Start out with an attractive, healthy African violet that can immediately cheer up your home with magnificent blossoms.

Plant features such as symmetry, color of the foliage, spotted leaves, disease, and the presences of insects should be scrutinized when selecting plants. Be selective to reduce the possibility of numerous problems later.

Question 14 **What can I do to make one of my favorite plants, which I have had for years, look attractive again? The problem is several of the older, lower leaves in the bottom two rows have dropped off.**

When your favorite African violet has become old, with all or most of the mature leaves gone from the lower row of leaves (rosette), it is an easy task to restore the plant to its former beauty. The main trunk of the plant is exposed because of the loss of all the lower leaves causing the plant to look like a palm tree. This condition is referred to as a "necky" plant. Three techniques can be used to revitalize a necky African violet: (1) You can take the plant from the pot and remove some of the potting mixture from the bottom of the root mass (soil ball). This allows you to set the plant deeper into the pot so that the lowest rows of leaves are just poking over the rim of the pot. Then fill up around the neck of the plant with a fresh potting mixture. (2) Another way to solve the problem is simply remove the plant from the pot, slice the plant off barely above the potting mixture, lightly scrape the stalk, and then root the top portion of the plant in water or a potting mixture. Remove most the foliage before trying to root the plant. (3) A third approach to the problem is to leave the plant in the pot and root the lower part of the main stem without severely disturbing the plant. To do this obtain some sphagnum peat moss and pack it loosely around the lower, exposed trunk. The peat moss should be pre-soaked in water for 48 hours before using it. Wrap a piece of saran wrap (from the kitchen) tightly around the peat so the moisture in it will not be able to evaporate. Anchor the saran wrap in the potting mixture. I read an article that suggested using a Styrofoam cup and altering it so it could be placed around the neck (stalk) of the plant. Fill it with the potting mixture and keeping it moist should work just as well as the saran wrap. Check the peat moss periodically and if it is drying add more water to the peat moss. Small rootlets should form in about three to six weeks. At the end of eight weeks the peat moss should be full of roots. The plant is now ready for repotting. Slice the stem off at potting mixture level and carefully unwrap the saran wrap from around the peat moss full of new roots. Put the peat moss with its root mass into a new pot and add more potting mixture as needed.

All three methods will cause a set back to the growth of the plant but it will recover in a few short weeks and begin producing those lovely blossoms again.

Question 15 African violets are on sale all the time in the grocery stores. What guidelines should I use for selecting a plant for a gift?

Most of the time the African violets found in the grocery stores have come from large growers, such as the Optimara Violets from Holtkamp Greenhouses, Inc. in Nashville, Tennessee. If the store is taking proper care of the violets after delivery they will make a very nice gift for a friend. See Q&A #13 for additional information.

Question 16 A year ago my plant had gorgeous violet colored flowers. Today they are sort of a reddish color. Has my African violet sported and can I claim it as a new variety?

The flower color of a single plant will not always remain the same. It can be very frustrating to African violet hobbyists when the color will not remain constant.

Cultural practices will play an important role in the exact color of the flowers. Type and amount of plant food available, light intensity, and potting mixture conditions—all have a definite effect on flower color. To maintain flowers of the same color you must give the plant the same care all the time. Any changes in your cultural practices may cause a change in the flower color of your favorite plant.

The pigments which give the flowers their purple, red, pink, and blue color are all sensitive to the pH conditions in the plant cells where the pigment is located. The interaction of the pigments with the pH in the cells is the reason for the flower color changing on an individual plant.

You may not claim the plant as a new variety because the varying flower color is not a permanent change in the plant's features.

Question 17 **What is a boy plant and a girl plant?**
These two terms were coined to distinguish different leaf types from one another. The first African violet plants had leaves that were solid green. When one plant, whose parent was named 'Blue Boy,' sported a leaf with a white discoloration at the base of the leaf, a new name was needed to classify this unusual foliage. The term girl-type was selected and since then the boy-type and girl-type nomenclature has been used to describe the two different leaf characteristics.

Do not confuse girl leaves with the variegated designation used for African violet leaves. Variegated leaves have various degrees of white or other colored splotches disbursed over the leaves.

Question 18 **The shapes of the African violet leaves really show a lot of variation. Would you list the different leaf types for me?**
They are: cupped, holly, variegated, plain (tailored), heart, round, bustle, Supreme (Amazon & DuPont), longifolia (spider), ovate, spooned, pointed, compound (bustle, piggyback, or wasp), trumpeted, and quilted. To this list let's add some of the various types of leaf margins: fluted, fringed, ruffled, scallop, serrated, and wavy. The variety of leaf shapes and leaf edges has added to the popularity of African violets.

Question 19 **Does the word "variegated" refer to the two colors seen in many African violet blossoms?**
No. This term is reserved for use in discussing African violets with individual leaves displaying two different colors, usually white and green. Other combinations of colors which occur in the green leaves are: rose, red, pink, cream, light yellow, chartreuse, or dark green. Blossoms displaying two or more different colors are referred to as being bi-colored.

Melvin J. Robey

LEAF TYPES

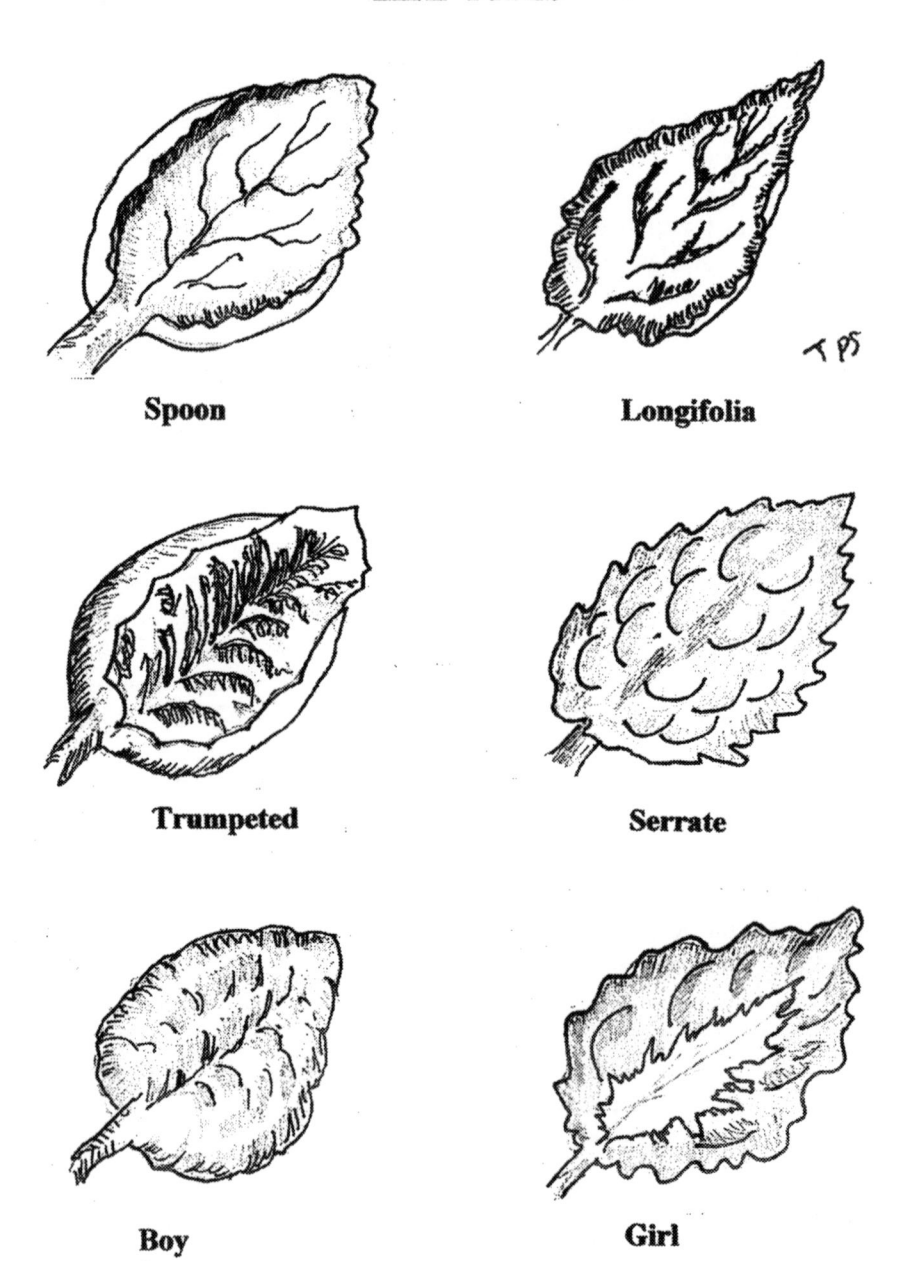

Spoon

Longifolia

Trumpeted

Serrate

Boy

Girl

African Violets Back to the Basics

Geneva Blossom

Fringed Edged Blossom

Star Blossom

Fantasy Blossom

Wasp Blossom

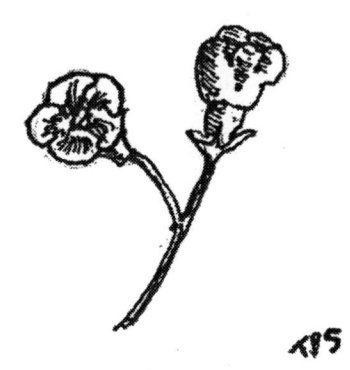

Bell Blossom

Question 20   Do variegated plants require special care?

Two things should be watched closely when seeing to the needs of these special plants. Give them as strong a light as possible. Do not expose them to so much natural sunlight that the leaves begin to sunburn. Feed them regularly with a fertilizer low in nitrogen; occasionally it is okay to use a fertilizer lacking nitrogen. Three examples of plant food to use on variegated plants are: 0-15-14, 3-12-6, and 5-50-17.

Question 21   Do the plants producing the double petal blossoms offer any advantages over growing the standard flowering types?

Yes. The main one being the double blossoms are more showy flowers, causing the plant to be more attractive. Another important feature of these plants is their blossoms last much longer on the plant. This gives these African violets the appearance of producing more blossoms than the older, standard (5 petals) flowering African violets.

Question 22   I have a very limited amount of space in my small apartment but would like to grow some plants. Are there any African violets that would fit on small windowsills?

Whenever a person wants to cheer up their apartment but does not want to overcrowd it with a lot of big plants they should consider growing the smallest beauties of all—the miniature African violets. These delicate plants require a minimum amount of space to produce gorgeous blossoms for your enjoyment. Since they never get any larger than six inches in diameter they will fit into almost any space you have available for a plant or two.

Question 23   What about the flowering of miniature African violets? Are the blossoms more or less in number than the regular African violets?

Miniatures are similar to the standard plants; some varieties produce more blossoms than others. In comparison, I would have to say they flower just as much as the standard African violet plants.

Question 24   I have several standard and miniature African violets and have noticed the miniatures do not grow as fast as the standards. Is this normal?

Yes. It is natural for these smaller plants to be slower in their growth. If the growth seems to be unusually slow then check your cultural practices. Make sure you have been taking care of these miniature plants properly. If you do they will make a lovely addition to your home.

African Violets Back to the Basics

A beautiful flowering African violet catches the eye of this lovely lady. (MJR)

Question 25 **Is it natural for several suckers to develop on my miniature varieties? It seems I am always removing them from my plants.**

Miniature African violets do have a tendency to form suckers. Be very watchful for the development of these new shoots and remove them as quickly as you are positive they are suckers and not flower buds. Do not forget to root them after their removal so you have new plants to give to your friends.

Question 26 **How difficult are miniatures to care for in a natural light?**

When grown in natural light more attention must be paid to these plants. They need a steady source of light, which is difficult to obtain in a windowsill. To overcome this problem your watering techniques, fertilizer program, and other cultural practices have to be done properly. Your best bet is to grow miniature African violets under fluorescent lighting whenever possible. Rotating the plants from under the lights to favorite spots in your home is a good idea.

Question 27 **Can I successfully grow miniatures under fluorescent lights?**

Yes. They will do as well under artificial lighting as any other African violet. The lights should be six to eight inches from the tops of these little plants. If you are growing miniature and standards under the same lights then elevate the miniatures to the correct distance from the lights.

Question 28   When buying miniature plants do I have a wide choice in blossom color and leaf types?

Any feature you find in a standard African violet is available in a miniature plant. All the leaf types are available and so are the single, double, & semi-double blossoms—all the interesting types are yours for the choosing.

RESTING PERIOD

Question 29   What do people mean when talking about their African violets are going through a "resting period" each year?

After an African violet plant has spent most of the year producing gorgeous blossoms it is not uncommon for them to stop producing flowers for a short time. This non-blooming period is called the resting period. It should never last for more than a few short weeks. The purpose of this resting stage is to allow the plants to revitalize themselves and prepare for another year of blooming.

Question 30   Is a resting period necessary for the health of an African violet after a year of heavy flowering?

A resting period allowing the plants to regain their strength after each burst of blossoms is not necessary. African violets in their native surroundings in Africa, bloom year round without any adverse effect on the plants.

African violets should flower year round in your home if you are taking good care of them. The fertilizer, water, and light requirements must meet the plants needs for them to develop beautiful blossoms all the time.

Question 31   My plant has been flowering heavily for several months and I would like to force it into a rest period. How should I do it and when should it be done?

You are going to penalize a plant that has been constantly performing for you. If this is really what you want to do then follow these procedures: withhold fertilizer from the plant, give it less water, and remove any flower stalks as they begin to develop. The best time of the year to force a plant into a rest period is during the hotter summer months. This allows the plant to come back and burst into full bloom during the winter months when you need something bright and cheerful to get you through those longer winter days.

Question 32 **What techniques can I use to cause the individual blossoms on my African violets to be bigger?**

One way to accomplish this is to force them into a resting period or buy some of the varieties available that produce larger blossoms.

FLOWERING

Question 33 **Some of my African violets flower profusely while other plants seem to lack any desire to produce flowers. What am I doing wrong or is this just a way African violets flower?**

It is not uncommon to have an African violet that occasionally does not bloom as profusely as the rest of the plants in the home. Treat it tenderly, just as if it was one of your prize bloomers. If after several months of this loving care it still has not begun producing flowers you might as well get rid of it, unless you like its green foliage. This plant can be added to a planter with foliage plants and its occasional flower will add a nice splash of color to the planter.

The cultivar of African violet will greatly influence the flowering of the plant. Some plants are profuse bloomers while others develop larger than normal flowers but fewer in numbers. Age of a plant has lot to do with its ability flower. Do not forget when a new plant is first brought home it must undergo the necessary physiological changes to adapt to its new home. This usually means less flowers than you would normally expect. After a plant adjusts to its new environment it will begin flowering again.

Question 34 **In our home during the winter months the humidity drops to about 25%. Does this have anything to do with why my plants will not bloom?**

Yes. African violets like the humidity to be high, but it is difficult to keep it above 30 to 35 percent in most homes during the colder winter days. Low humidity causes the plants to produce fewer blossoms as you have already noticed. Another problem is the shorter winter days lower the light intensity, which may be part of the reason why the plants will not flower for you.

Question 35 **I moved my plants into the kitchen window located beside my gas range. In a very short time the new flower buds began dropping off as they formed. Any ideas as to what my problem may be?**

African violets are very sensitive to the air around them. If there is any gas fumes reaching the plants then you can be sure the problem is polluted air circulating around them. Another possibility is there was a temperature change from where you were previously keeping the plants to where they are now located. Any sudden temperature changes will cause the flower buds to drop off. Incidentally if you ever hear the term "blast" in connection with flower buds it means the same thing as "falling off."

Question 36 **I have been told if I pinch off the new buds on my plants I can expect an increase in the number of blossoms developing later. Is this fact or fiction?**

Fact. Someone is telling you the truth about a procedure called disbudding. The process is a simple one. When the flower stalk bearing the buds is about 1 to 1¼ inches long, use sharp scissors and snip it off. In less than five weeks you should see two or more flower stalks developing from around the base of the one you snipped off. If you really want a showy plant for some special occasion, disbudding is the secret to obtaining a gorgeous plant. Removal of the flower stalks should be done six to eight weeks ahead of the time you want the African violets to really put on a flowery display.

Question 37 **What are the yellow nodules in the center of the flower?**

These structures are part of the male portion of the flower. Their botanical name is stamen. It is in these sac-like pods where the male pollen is produced and one-half of the necessary genetic information is stored for future plant development. You should notice some plants have an extra set of stamens, a common characteristic of plants with semi-double and double blossoms.

Question 38 **I have noticed the semi-double and double blossoms on my plants have an extra set of yellow stamens. Is this unusual?**

No. It is normal for this to occur in these types of blossoms. If you were to have an extra set of stamens in the standard five-petal blossom then you would have an unusual plant.

Question 39 **Many of my African violets have from five to seven and even ten individual flower petals. Are these blossoms mutants?**

The first African violets brought to the Untied States had five single petals. Then several years later blossoms with anywhere from six to ten petals started showing up. These were sports (mutants), which nature created for the enjoyment of enthusiastic African violet hobbyists.

Question 40 **Please explain the differences between the three basic flowering types: standard, semi-double, and double?**

The standard (often called tailored) blossoms have five petals, divided into two upper petals and three lower petals. A semi-double blossom contains anywhere from six to nine petals. The extra petals form a tuft in the center of the blossoms. Double blossoms are composed of ten petals that give the

African Violets Back to the Basics

flower a very full appearance. The semi-double and double blossoms are in great demand because of their attractiveness.

Question 41   I have seen a wide assortment of flower shapes at a specialty greenhouse where I buy my African violets. Could you tell me the names of some of the common shapes and colors of the blossoms?

Here is a partial list of the different blossom types:

Bi-color:	each petal on the blossom displays two distinct colors
Fantasy:	each petal on the flower has a speckled appearance
Geneva:	the petals are one color, with white edges
Multi-colored:	petals on blossoms have three or more colors present
Poppy:	the throat or center of the blossom is bright red with outer portions of the petals white in color
Pinwheel:	white petals with a colored stripe down the center of each petal

Some others are wasp, holly, edged, chimera, star, fringed and bell.

Question 42   Are the star shaped blossoms common in the world of African violets?

It is not unusual to see them and there are several varieties on the market from which to choose. Your best place to buy them is from the African violet specialty growers advertising in the African Violet Society of America magazine. You seldom see them in the stores around town. The star shaped blossom is a sport which developed from the standard blossoms common in the early varieties of African violets.

Question 43   I pollinated a couple of blossoms on my African violet and the seedpods have begun to develop. How long will it take for the seeds to be ready for collecting and planting?

The length of time you will have to wait will depend upon which size African violet you are working with. As a general rule of thumb expect the miniatures to produce mature seed in three months and all the other African violets to take five to six months. Watch the seedpod as it develops and when it turns brown and starts to shrivel up it should be removed. Store the pods in an envelope for two to four weeks to allow the seed to complete its maturation. Then you can plant the seed anytime you are ready.

Question 44   How many seeds will develop in a seedpod?

This will vary but usually you can expect in the neighborhood of five hundred seeds per pod. If you were to weigh the seeds you would discover it would take 750,000 seeds to weigh a single ounce.

CHAPTER 3

PLANT FOOD ESSENTIAL FOR HEALTHY PLANTS

Question 45 **Should I use a liquid fertilizer or the dry, granular fertilizer I have seen for sale at the store?**
It does not make any difference to the plant whether you use a liquid or a granular fertilizer. Choose the one you feel is most convenient for you. Many hobbyists prefer the liquid or solid plant food dissolved in water. This allows the plants to be fed each time they are watered. A liquid fertilizer is available more quickly to the plant but its availability is short lived. This is okay if you understand this and apply the liquid fertilizer on a regular schedule.

With a granular plant food once you put it on the potting mixture it will begin to dissolve and release slowly to the plants. Eventually the plant will use all of it and more plant food will need to be added again, just like a liquid plant food. Consider mixing in a granular fertilizer when preparing a potting mixture and switch to a liquid once the plant has become established in the pot.

Question 46 **Salt has been accumulating on the rims of my neighbor's pots. They water the plants from the bottom and also use wicks. Does this have any effect on the salt build up on the pots?**
What you are seeing is a classic example of improper watering. As the water moves up thought the potting mixture it dissolves any salts present and carries them to the surface of the potting mixture and onto pot rim (primarily when using porous clay pots). The salts are then concentrated in these areas as the water evaporates, causing the white crust to form.

Question 47 **What can be done to solve the problem after a white, salty crust has formed on the potting soil surface and rim of the pot?**

First, change watering habits. Start watering from the top frequently enough to keep the salts washed down into the potting mixture. Be sure to let some of the water drip out the bottom, allowing some of the accumulated salts to be washed out of the potting mixture. To restore the potted plant to a more acceptable appearance use a spoon to remove approximately one-quarter inch of the surface of the potting mixture. Replace the white, crusty potting mix with a fresh clean mixture. Take a damp cloth and wipe the crusted salt from the rim is the best solution for cleaning up the unsightliness of the pot itself.

Question 48 **Could you tell me how an African violet uses all those different nutrients found in a fertilizer?**

The three primary nutrients you should know how the plant uses are: nitrogen, phosphorus, and potassium. Understanding how these nutrients affect the growth and flowering of your African violets will help improve your green thumb reputation among your friends.

Nitrogen

This important plant food, when present in large amounts, causes the plants to grow rapidly. For this reason a good supply should be present when the young plants, from cuttings or seeds, are first developing but have yet to mature enough to produce flowers. As these young plants mature then the application of nitrogen should be reduced. Excess nitrogen suppresses flower formation.

Nitrogen gives the plant leaves and stems the nice green color you enjoy so much. Too little nitrogen in the potting mixture causes the leaves to turn yellowish, ruining the lovely appearance of your Africans violets.

One additional fact you need to be aware of is the effect nitrogen has on variegated African violets. Too much nitrogen applied to these plants will cause the beautiful variegation in the leaves to disappear, causing the plants to have all green leaves. This should not be a problem once the plants mature and you reduce the amount of nitrogen you apply. Variegation will return to the leaves when less nitrogen is available.

Phosphorus

An adequate supply of this nutrient in the potting mixture is essential for the development of healthy roots. It is also an important nutrient needed for flower and seed formation.

Potassium

The exact function of this plant food has not been determined. It seems to move from cell to cell in the plant without ever becoming attached to anything. One fact known about potassium is its presence improves a plant's resistance to diseases.

*****

Note: In Pauline Bartholomew book, *Growing to Show*, she succinctly shows what each of the three major nutrients provides to an African violet. "....nitrogen for foliage, phosphorus for floriferousness [flowering], and potassium for general health [of the plants]."

*****

There are thirteen other plant foods used by African violets but the three discussed above should give you the necessary information you need for growing African violets. Most of the nutrients are usually present in small quantities in the fertilizers you are using and should meet the needs of your plants.

PLANT FOOD FIGURES

Question 49 **I have been looking at the label on a box of fertilizer and was wondering what the numbers 12-36-14 are referring to. Is this the amount of plant food contained in the box of fertilizer? And, are these numbers always the same on all fertilizer packages?**

You have come close to figuring out what the numbers represent. They actually tell you the percent of nitrogen (12%), phosphorus (36%), and potassium (14%) contained in the fertilizer. The answer to your second question is no, all fertilizers do not have the same grade (% nitrogen, % phosphorus, % potassium). Each manufacturer develops their individual blend of African violet food and packages it for sale.

Question 50 **Please list some of the different types of fertilizers that are available for use on my plants.**

In checking the advertisements in the *African Violet Magazine* the following types of plant food were found to be available. There are many others not listed here. This list will provide you with representative sampling of fertilizers for African violets.

Fertilizer	% Nitrogen	% Phosphorus	% Potassium
Spoonit	18	20	16
Plant Marvel	12	31	14
Alaska Fish Fertilizer	5	1	1
Sturdy	0	15	14
Dyna-Gro	7	9	5
Dyna-Gro	3	12	6
Dyna-Gro	9	3	6

Dyna-Gro	0	0	3
Mag-Amp	7	40	6
Peter's Violet Special	12	36	14
Peter's Variegated Special	5	50	17

Question 51 **If I buy a ten ounce container of 20-20-20 fertilizer, how much of the material in the container is actually plant food?**

It is very easy to calculate the answer to your question. First add the three figures together and this will tell you the percentage of the material in the container, which is actual plant food. Doing this you find 60% of the ten ounces will be used as plant food by your African violets. The final step in finding an answer to your question is to multiply 60% times ten ounces. This gives you a figure of six ounces, which is the actual plant food in the box which the African violets can utilize. The other 40% is composed of "carrier" material, which holds the nitrogen, phosphorus, and potassium until they are dissolved in the potting mixture and used by the plants.

Question 52 **When I add up the percent of plant food in the container at the store it never equals 100 percent. How come?**

To answer your question let's assume you have a container of a popular granular fertilizer with 5% nitrogen, 10% phosphorus, and 10% potassium. Adding the percentages gives you a total of 25%. This figure will never be equal to 100% in any plant food. The reason is the fertilizer must be diluted with some sort of inert material so the plant food can be packaged in a form acceptable to the plants. If all the material were 100% fertilizer it would be so salty it would damage your African violets. Even when the fertilizer is diluted it is still salty enough to be harmful to the plants if it is not applied properly.

FERTILIZERS INFLUENCE THE PLANTS DEVELOPMENT

Question 53 **Does the type of fertilizer I use have any influence on how well my African violets bloom?**

Definitely. When you have a plant that is mature and producing numerous flowers you should use a plant food low in nitrogen, high in phosphorus, and high in potassium. Something like a 3-12-6 or 5-50-17 works well. If you use a fertilize high in nitrogen, like 18-20-16, you will force the plant to produce leaves and green coloring which will reduce the number of blossoms your African violets will produce.

Question 54 A friend warned me not to overfeed my plants with a fertilizer high in nitrogen. Now I am wondering why it would hurt my plants. Can you tell me?

Yes. Nitrogen is the primary nutrient causing rapid shoot growth in plants, at the expense of the development of a healthy root system and the formation of blossoms. The rapid growth of the stems and leaves causes them to be weak and susceptible to diseases. This type of growth also distracts from the overall appearance of your African violets.

Question 55 How can I tell when my African violets are not being fed enough nitrogen?

One of the first and most difficult nitrogen deficiency symptoms to identify is a stunting of the plant's growth. The African violet will lose its vigor, failing to develop as quickly as you anticipate it should. If nitrogen continues being withheld from the plant for a long time the leaves will start to turn yellow, first along the margins then the entire leaf turns yellow, eventually dropping off. Being on a regular feeding program with a plant food containing nitrogen will steer you clear of this problem.

Question 56 I would like to feed my plants on a regular schedule so they have the necessary plant food available to keep them flowering year round. How is the best way to accomplish this?

A good way to accomplish your goal is to dissolve the fertilizer in the water you use for your African violets. This way every time you water your plants they will receive a little plant food. If you do this it is a good idea to cut the fertilizer rate in half from what is recommended on the fertilizer container. Also, be sure to water from the top and to allow the excess water to drip out the bottom of the container at each watering.

Be careful not to get any water on the leaves. It will leave a white residue and could cause the plant cells to die where the fertilizer and water mixture dried on the leaves.

Question 57 A favorite plant of mine has quit flowering after several months of producing blossoms. My question is this, should I fertilize the plant to try to force it into flowering again?

Definitely not, you will do more harm to the plant than good. While African violets do not need a resting period between bursts of blossoms it is not a good idea to force a resting violet into flowering by applying a fertilizer. Give the plant plenty of light, water it when needed, and it will begin flowering again for you. When it does, feed it a fertilizer low in nitrogen and high in phosphorus and potassium.

PLANT FOOD FACTS

Question 58 **What is the difference between a trace element, a micronutrient, and a major nutrient?**

All the terms are referring to the plant nutrients African violets need to remain healthy and flowering. Three terms—trace, minor, and micro—are used for a category of plants foods used in very small amounts by the plants. Do not under estimate their importance because of the terms used to categorize them. Without them African violets will not do very well. Major nutrients are those used in large amounts by the plant.

NUTRIENTS USED BY PLANTS

Major Nutrients	Micronutrients*
Nitrogen	Iron
Phosphorus	Zinc
Potassium	Copper
Sulfur	Boron
Magnesium	Manganese
Calcium	Molybdenum
	Chlorine

* also referred to as trace nutrients and minor nutrients

Question 59 **I did not know vitamins were good for African violets until a friend told me about them. Is the plant's growth improved or do the vitamins increase flowering?**

One of the great myths in the plant world: Vitamins, when applied to the potting mixture, will be utilized by the plant for its growth and in producing flowers. Fact: the African violet plant (or any other plant) has never been known to use a vitamin, when added to the potting mixture, in any of its metabolic processes for plant growth or flower production.

There is one way the vitamins, when added to the potting mixture, aid in the development of healthy African violets. Tiny microorganisms, such as bacteria, found in the potting mixture use the vitamins as a food source. The introduction of the vitamins into the potting mixture provides the microorganisms with an additional food source, enabling them to break down the organic matter and fertilizers, increasing the availability of nutrients to the African violets.

Question 60 **Is it true chemical fertilizers are dangerous to the plants and only organic plant food should be used?**

There is no truth to the statement chemical fertilizers, when applied properly, are harmful to African violets or any other type of plants. I have been growing plants for several years and have never had a single plant die due to using a chemically manufactured plant food. The only way these materials will harm your plants is if you do not follow the directions on the label when feeding your plants. Too much plant food, caused my over applying the material to the plants, can damage and even kill your plants. Also if you accidentally spill any of the fertilizer on a plant you will damage it. Be sure to follow the labeled directions which come with the boxed or bagged plant food and you should not encounter any problems.

Question 61   At a recent party I listened to two of my friends discussing the merits of natural organic fertilizers and chemical fertilizers. What is the difference?

A natural organic fertilizer is a plant food which is produced by Mother Nature. The more common animal manures are often processed and sold as natural organic plant foods. Three of other examples of natural organic fertilizers are: bone meal, dried animal blood, and fish emulsions.

A chemical fertilizer is prepared by a fertilizer company where specific plant food elements are combined and packaged for use on African violets. These types of plant foods usually have a high percent of nitrogen, phosphorus, and potassium present in them. Examples of these are plant foods with the following fertilizer grades shown on the package: 20-20-20, 5-50-17, 7-9-5, 12-36-14, and 15-30-15.

Question 62   Should a granular fertilizer be mixed into the special potting soil I am preparing?

It is okay to mix a granular fertilizer into the potting mixture to enrich it. You will still need to periodically add fertilizer as the plants mature. One problem with pre-mixing fertilizers with the potting mixture is a tendency to get to much plant food concentrated in the potting mixture. This can damage the new roots because of their sensitivity to high concentrations of fertilizer salts in the potting mixture.

Question 63   Should I follow the manufacturers recommended rates for a fertilizer when I am feeding my plants?

Always—I repeat—always follow the labeled directions which come with any chemical you use. This eliminates most of the accidents before they have a chance to occur. It is not unusual for experienced African violet hobbyists to slightly reduce the rates of fertilizer used on their plants. This helps ensure against any fertilizer damage to their favorite African violets. Never increase the fertilizer rate beyond what is recommended on the package or container.

Question 64 **Does the potting soil I buy at the garden center already have plant food in it?**

All soils and potting mixtures, regardless of where you find them, do have some of the essential plant nutrients in them. African violet potting mixtures usually do not have any plant food added to the mixture prior to packaging it for sale in the stores. The amount of naturally occurring plant food found in these potting mixtures is usually very small and not enough to sustain a plant for very long. You may mix a small amount of fertilizer in the potting mixture prior to potting your African violet. After putting your plants in a new potting mixture I would wait about seven days before starting a fertilizer program. This brief period gives the plants a chance to adapt to their new home.

FEEDING CORRECTLY HELPS

Question 65 **I was told to feed a "Complete" fertilizer at least once a year to my plants. I cannot find a plant food by this name anywhere. What should I do?**

A complete fertilizer is not referring to any particular brand or product but to all fertilizer products containing nitrogen, phosphorus, and potassium. If a plant food is missing any one of these three nutrients then it is not a complete fertilizer. You will have healthier African violets if you fed them a complete fertilizer more than once a year. I would suggest feeding them a complete fertilizer at least twice a month, except during the winter when the growth of the plants has slowed down. You should also consider mixing the fertilizer in with the water used to keep the potting mixture moist.

Question 66 **I have heard of a special plant food for variegated African violets. Is this fact or fiction?**

It is true there are special plant foods available for variegated plants. The analysis will be low in nitrogen (example: 5-50-17) and if you have a large number of variegated plants you should buy it. If this exact fertilizer is not available then pick another one which is low in nitrogen and you should not have any problems with your variegated plants.

Low nitrogen is desirable when feeding the variegated leaf varieties. Feeding these plants a fertilizer high in nitrogen will cause the leaves to lose their variegation and you will end up with plants having all green leaves. Once the nitrogen available to the plants is reduced the leaf variegation will return.

Question 67 **My favorite variegated plant now has leaves that are now almost 100% green. I have been watering the plant faithfully and it gets plenty of light. I fertilize every two weeks with a 20-20-20 plant**

food mixed with the water. Any ideas on why the leaves are no longer variegated?

It sounds as if you are too good to your favorite plant, when it comes feeding time. This plant along with any of the other variegated African violets should not be fed a fertilizer that is high in nitrogen. An excessive amount of this plant nutrient causes the variegated leaves to convert to an all green color. To avoid this problem in the future use a fertilizer low in nitrogen and high in phosphorus and potassium. Examples of this type of plant food are: 5-50-17 and 3-12-6.

On a positive note, the leaves will gradually revert back to their natural variegation once the correct plant food is used.

Question 68 What good does pulverized egg shells do when mixed into a soil used for potting African violets? I have a friend who does this all the time and swears by it as the reason for always having beautiful plants.

Eggshells are a good source of calcium, one of the important nutrients needed by African violets. By pulverizing the shells, decomposition occurs more quickly, releasing the calcium for the plant to absorb from the potting mixture. While the extra calcium does help improve the general appearance of African violets I would have to believe your friend's success at growing beautiful plants lies in the excellent care they are receiving.

Question 69 Will growing African violets under artificial lighting have any effect on how much plant food needs to be given to the plants?

Yes. If you leave the lights on for 12 to 16 hours a day the plants will be growing rapidly. In order to remain healthy while developing so quickly they will require a steady supply of food. Do not overlook this fact or you will reduce the effectiveness of the special lighting you are giving your African violets, which is causing them to be flowering beauties.

Question 70 I have mixed a fertilizer into the water I plan on using. Is it okay to spray the solution directly onto the leaves of my African violets?

Foliar feeding your plants will not harm them unless you are careless. There are several precautions you should be aware of when applying plant food as a spray onto your African violets. They are:
1. Do not use cold water, it should be at room temperature
2. Do not add too much fertilizer to the solution; excessive amounts of fertilizer will cause damage to the leaves
3. Good air circulation around the plants is important

4. Mist the plants with the fertilizer solution; do not drench them with the solution
5. Keep the plants out of direct sunlight until the leaves are dry
6. Pick out a fertilizer you want to use and test it on one or two of your plants before treating all of the plants in your collection
7. Foliar applications of plant food can stain the leaves
8. Spraying plants when humidity is lowest will allow the leaves to dry quickly, thus reducing the chance of leaf spotting
9. Choose a fertilizer especially developed for foliar feeding of plants

Question 71 **What does foliar feeding of plants accomplish that other methods of fertilizing don't?**

If you are on a regular fertilizing schedule then foliar applications are of little benefit to your plants. Plants that have not been fertilized for a long time can get a quick boost by spraying a foliar fertilizer solution on their leaves. Sick looking leaves will perk up quickly and the general appearance of the plants will improve temporarily. To return the plants to a healthy appearance apply a fertilizer to the potting mixture at the same time so the roots can begin absorbing the plant food.

Question 72 **Is there any kind of fertilizer routine that should be followed for feeding my plants?**

African violets are similar to people when it comes to being fed. These lovely plants prefer to be fed on a regular bases, for example every two weeks. Feeding the plants large amounts of fertilizer irregularly is not good for their health or ability to produce flowers.

Question 73 **When should you fertilize a newly potted African violet?**

I would wait a minimum of one week and sometimes up to two weeks before feeding plants that have just been potted. Giving the plants a chance to overcome the shock of being potted is a good idea if you want to see it flower quickly. Also, by waiting you give the roots a chance to develop and adapt to their new home. The first feeding should be at only half of the recommended strength found on the fertilizer container. A small amount of fertilizer mixed in with the new potting mixture will be enough to sustain the plants until the first regular feeding.

CHAPTER 4

POTTING MIXTURES: KEY TO BEING SUCCESSFUL

African violet hobbyists often use the term soil when asking questions and/or discussing the mixtures used for growing their plants. When writing about potted plants I always struggle with the term soil. My educational background tells me a soil has three basic components: sand, silt, and clay. The type of soil will vary depending on the percentages of each present. Anything else like organic matter (peat), vermiculite, and perlite modifies the various physical and chemical characteristics of a soil. For example, organic matter increases the water holding capacity of the soil and also improves its aeration or ability to hold more air.

Based on this background information, I always try to use the term potting mixture or growing medium when discussing the contents in the pots in which the African violets are growing. One exception is I will use the term soil if a true soil is being used, which is rare among African violet hobbyists. Sometimes in a sentence or paragraph it becomes awkward when having to use the term potting mixture when the shorter-term soil would appear to be a better choice. But then I would not be presenting the information correctly.

Question 74 **Is it okay to use the special African violet soil mixtures sold at most of the garden centers?**
Chances are good you will be able to grow gorgeous African violets in these pre-packaged potting mixtures. Often they have been sieved through a screen to remove all the coarser organic material. This may cause the mixture to contain too many fine sized particles, allowing it to pack to tightly in the pot for good, healthy root growth. To overcome this problem add shredded peat, vermiculite, or perlite to the potting mixture.

Question 75   Bugs seem to be a big problem with the African violets in my friend's home and I am worried about getting them on my plants. What are the chances there are bugs in the special potting mixture I bought?

Usually the potting mixtures in pre-packaged bags sold at the stores have been steam sterilized to kill the bugs, weeds, and nematodes. If the packagers did a good job you do not need to worry about anything. However, it does not hurt to be cautious and sterilize the potting mixture when you get it home. This way you will know it has been done properly and you will not have to be concerned about bringing any bugs into your home.

Question 76   What causes the surface of the soil in my pots to become moldy?

Whenever you keep the potting mixture to wet and have poor air circulation around your plants there is an excellent chance you will get mold forming on the surface of the potting mixture. Check the potting mixture before watering, making sure the surface is dry and the plants actually need watering. A fan set to blow a gentle breeze above the plant tops will help reduce the chances of stale air contributing to the problem.

Question 77   I know the soil in a pot serves as a base to support my African violets so they stand up tall and beautiful but what else does the soil do for a plant?

The potting mix acts primarily as a medium providing an environment for the roots to grow and to support the parts of the plant growing above the potting mixture. You have already mentioned one of the four basic functions of the potting mixture (that of anchoring the plant) so let's look at the other three important features of a good mixture. The plant's food is stored in the potting mixture, being held by the individual particles until the roots remove the nutrients for the plants use. A loose potting mixture will have plenty of microscopic pores (spaces) where oxygen and water are stored. These microscopic reservoirs are essential to your African violets health. For this reason you should always use a mixture that is loose and high in organic material.

FOUR FUNCTIONS OF POTTING MIXTURE
1. Allow the roots to anchor the plant
2. Hold water in pore spaces
3. Hold air in pore spaces
4. Hold plant nutrients

Question 78   **How can I keep the soil from washing through the drain hole in the bottom of my pots?**

Prior to putting anything into the pot you should cover the drain hole to prevent the potting mixture from washing through. Anytime I break one of my porous clay pots I take a hammer and bust it up into small pieces and save them. When I pot a plant I can place these broken pieces (chards) in the bottom of the pot to prevent the potting mixture from washing through the drain hole. Another item which works well for this job is Styrofoam. Pieces of Styrofoam cups will do just as good of job as pieces of broken clay pots. Using Styrofoam also reduces the weight of the potted plant—if this is a consideration.

Question 79   **What is a garden loam?**

Usually when an African violet hobbyist is talking about garden loam they are referring to a dark colored soil high in organic material and humus. The actual composition of the material will vary considerably but it will always contain a high amount of clay and silt along with the organic material. The soil from a compost pile is often referred to as a garden loam.

Question 80   **Is garden loam a good soil mix for African violets?**

In my opinion it is not suitable for use as a potting mixture. I do not even consider it as one of the ingredients to use in a special mixture for any of my plants. There are a few African violet growers who like to use garden loam and are successful. I recommend to beginners to avoid using garden loam until you have some experience with African violets. Those who are most successful have spend many years developing their understanding of the needs of the African violet plant when grown in a garden loam.

If you elect to use a garden loam which has not been sterilized you are leaving the door wide open for an invasion by insects, weeds, and diseases. Even if you sterilize the soil I would expect you to have a difficult time with your African violets.

Question 81   **In a magazine article on growing African violets a comment was made about the wet soil in a pot becoming sour. What did the writer mean by this comment?**

Often if an African violet has been planted in too large of a pot the potting mixture without roots actively growing in it will stay wet for longer periods of time. When this happens there is a low oxygen supply present, allowing undesirable microorganisms to flourish. These organisms produce toxic substances causing the potting mixture to have an unpleasant odor—thus the term "sour" is used to describe this condition.

When discussing the pH of a potting mixture the term sour is sometimes used to indicate an acid condition exists.

Question 82 **When repotting plants how should I pack the new soil down between the soil ball and sides of the pot?**

I have always used my fingers to push the potting mixture down into the pot. If you use a spoon handle, pencil, or some other object there is a good chance you will damage the plant unless you are very careful. The advantage to using your fingers is they are sensitive enough for you to be able to tell if too much pressure is being used to firm up the potting mixture. Too much pressure causes the potting mixture to become too compacted for good root development.

PREPARATION OF A POTTING MIX

Question 83 **What kind of problems will I be causing if I do not take the time to pre-soak the peat moss before using it in my potting soil?**

Dry peat moss will not mix as uniformly into the potting mixture as a pre-soaked peat moss. The first time you water the plants in this mixture a lot of the dry peat moss will float to the surface. If you accidentally water too much, allowing the water to flow over the rim, you will have a big mess. It will take the dry peat moss a long time to absorb moisture once it is in the mixture. This defeats one of the purposes of the peat moss, which is to store water for the roots to utilize when they need it. If the roots come into contact with the dried peat moss the delicate rootlets may die, causing a set back to the plant's development.

Question 84 **I am interested in concocting my own potting mixture. What special guidelines should I follow to make sure I have the best possible mixture?**

How good the potting mixture is will ultimately be determined by how well your African violets grow in it. To give the plants the best possible chance there are four basic guidelines you should follow when mixing ingredients together:

1. African violets like a mixture high in organic matter, therefore the potting mixture should contain 50 to 60 percent organic material—peat moss, seed hulls, bark, etc.
2. Check the potting mixture to determine its pH. It should be between 6.5 to 7.0. If it is not, then add the appropriate chemicals to bring the pH reading into this range.

3. The potting mixture should drain well yet have the capacity to retain sufficient water, nutrients, and air for good healthy plant growth. The addition of organic matter is a good way to ensure adequate drainage.
4. A source of food for the plants must be available in the potting mixture so plan on mixing a small amount of fertilizer into the potting mixture.

Question 85 **Is it okay to add plant food to my potting mixture before using it to pot my new plants?**

Yes. This is an excellent time to incorporate plant food into a potting mixture. Read the directions on the fertilizer container and be careful to follow them. You may wish to reduce the amount of plant food mixed into the potting mixture. The reason for this is you do not want to concentrate too much plant food in the potting mixture, causing salt damage to the tender roots of the African violets. Never increase the rates beyond what is recommended on the plant food container.

Question 86 **Are there any simple ways to sterilize my potting mixture?**

Yes. Three different techniques can be used to sterilize small amounts of potting mixture. Choose the one which is most convenient for you.

TECHNIQUE #1 BAKING
Steps to Follow
1. Moisten the potting mixture and place it in a shallow tray
2. Place the tray in the oven and bake the potting mixture for one hour at 212 degrees Fahrenheit
3. Remove the potting mixture from the oven and allow it to cool
4. Gases that escaped from the potting mixture are harmful to plants. Do not use the potting mixture for two weeks. Stir the mixture occasionally during this time to allow the gases to escape

TECHNIQUE #2 STEAM
Steps to Follow
1. Place the potting mixture in jars
2. Fill pressure cooker with approximately ½ inch of water
3. Put jars filled with potting mixture in pressure cooker and set pressure for 15 pounds; maintain pressure for thirty minutes
4. Remove jars and let them set, with lids off, for two weeks; stir occasionally to allow poisonous gases to escape

TECHNIQUE # 3 CHEMICAL
Steps to Follow
1. Sprinkle one quart of formaldehyde solution (1 pint 37% commercial formaldehyde to 4 gallons of water) on one square foot by six inches of potting mixture
2. Water liberally to wash chemical solution into the potting mixture
3. Tightly cover the potting mixture for 48 hours
4. Uncover the potting mixture and stir frequently to allow gases to escape
5. Wait at least two weeks before using the potting mixture; wait longer if you can still smell the formaldehyde fumes. These fumes are very toxic to African violets

Question 87 **How can I tell if the potting mixture I have prepared will be good for growing African violets?**

The best way to find out is to grow a plant in it, observing how well it does. There is a simple test you can perform in a matter of minutes and it will give you a general idea if your potting mix is a good one. It is called the "ball test."

Take a handful of the potting mixture you have prepared and dampen it so it is uniformly moist, but not saturated (dripping water). Squeeze it into as tight of ball as possible. Then open your hand and see if the ball stays tightly packed or if it has numerous cracks in it and tends to crumble apart easily. If it fits into the later case, then you probably have a good potting mixture for growing your plants. If the ball is still tightly packed add some more organic material to the mixture to loosen it up. A loose mixture will maintain a good balance of oxygen and water in the potting mixture where the roots must grow.

Question 88 **What are some examples of potting mixtures other African violet enthusiasts are using?**

These two are fairly representative of the types of mixes used by many hobbyists. Other ingredients can be added based on your personal experience or at the suggestion of another enthusiast. Not mention in the two examples here is the addition of any fertilizer.

Lyndon Lyon Greenhouses, Inc	Ednah Daw
3 parts sphagnum peat moss	from *How I Grow African Violets*
2 parts #2 coarse vermiculite	2 parts sphagnum peat moss
1 part coarse perlite	1 part vermiculite
<u>Note</u>: to this mix add sufficient fine dolomite lime to lower the pH to 6.6	1 part perlite
	½ part crushed charcoal
	½ part bone meal

Question 89 I have a question concerning the correct way to measure soils when mixing a special blend for African violets. Should each ingredient be weighted to ensure the correct proportions?

Probably the simplest and most efficient way to measure the ingredients you are mixing together is to use a cup or quart jar as a measuring tool. After measuring all the ingredients stir them together and you have prepared your potting mixture by using volume measurements.

If the potting mixture does not seem correct then add whichever ingredients you think are needed to make the potting mixture perfect. Keep a record of what you are using and the exact measurements of each ingredient. This will allow you to duplicate the potting mix and also make minor adjustments as needed.

Question 90 I am confused as to what I should buy for preparing my own special potting mixture. After listening to all my friends advice and reading up on the subject it appears anything will work. Is this a safe assumption?

It depends a lot upon the ingredients you have in mind when you say "anything." Some of the more common ingredients used in potting mixtures are: peat, perlite, vermiculite, sand, packaged African violet potting mixtures from the garden centers, and shredded bark. There are numerous materials not listed here which you may elect to try. The final test of your selection of ingredients will be how well your African violets do when grown in the mixture. Experiment with different potting mixtures, choosing the one which works best for you.

SALT PROBLEMS

Question 91 Once the sodium has accumulated in the soil and a white crust has formed is there anyway to purify the soil of the excess sodium and other salts?

Use a small spoon and carefully scrape the white crust off the potting mixture surface. Toss this toxic material in the garbage. After doing this carefully scrub the rim of the pot with plenty of water to remove the salts. By doing this you reduce the chances of any leaves, which touch the rim, from developing stem rot.

If you have a soft water conditioner hooked up in your home, use the water from an outside tap to ensure it is free of sodium. Pour several cups of this water on the top of the potting mixture, allowing it to drain through the mixture and out the drain hole into the sink. Do not reuse this leachate (water).

This process will get rid of most of the damaging sodium and salts from the potting mixture. The last step is to add fresh potting mixture to replace that which was scraped out.

Salt crust on the rim of a clay pot. (MJR)

Question 92   I just had a soft water conditioner installed in my home. Will the water still be okay for watering my plants?

Soft water conditioners improve the water in your home by removing the impurities (iron, calcium, magnesium, and other hard salts) and replacing them with sodium. This makes the water soft to your skin but the sodium can create a serious hazard to African violets. When sodium builds up in the potting mixture it retards the growth of plants. If on occasion you absolutely need to use soft water then go ahead. It will not hurt the African violets when used infrequently. The problem arises from continually using water high in sodium. This causes a sodium (salt) build up in the potting mixture. When this happens the plant is in trouble. (Note: Sodium will increase the pH into the 8.5 range or higher.)

Question 93   A white crust is forming on the soil surface of my potted African violets. What is causing this?

What you are seeing is an accumulation of excess salts on the potting mixture surface. You are either fertilizing too much or using water from a soft water conditioner (or both) and getting a build up of sodium and other salts. Another contributing factor would be if you always water from the bottom of the pot and never from the top.

Your plants will suffer if salts are allowed to continue to accumulate on the surface of the potting mixture and the rims of the pots. You should remedy this problem as soon as possible. Four quick points for you to consider are: (1) Do not use too much soft water, (2) frequently water from the top, (3) allow a small amount of the water to drain out of the pot, and (4) check your fertilizer schedule.

Question 94 **There is a rusty orange-reddish crust forming on the edge of my clay pots and on the soil surface. What is it?**

This is an accumulation of salts that has happened over a long period of time. The color is due to other impurities being present with the salt. The salt usually adheres to the rim of a clay pot so tightly it is necessary to repot the plant and toss the old one in the garbage. When this condition occurs it is the result of continually watering the plant and not allowing any of the water to drain out of the pot. As the potting mixture dries out, the salts move up to the surface of the potting mixture.

Question 95 **How does the high sodium [salt] content in the soil mixture actually harm African violets?**

The problem is not an internal one where the plant absorbs the sodium, then gets sick and dies. Just the opposite occurs. When sodium is in higher concentrations in the potting mixture than in the plant's cells it attracts the moisture from the plant's cells. This causes the moisture to move from the plant cells into the potting mixture. When this happens the cells become dehydrated, eventually drying up and then dying.

A LOOK AT pH

Question 96 **What is the meaning of the letters pH?**

Horticulturists and scientists use this letter designation, along with numbers, to explain to the gardener how acid or alkaline a soil or potting mixture is. Actually, it is a mathematical measurement of the quantity of hydrogen ions in the soil or potting mixture.

A potting mixture with a pH of 5.5 has a high concentration of hydrogen causing the potting mixture to be acid. African violets like a potting mixture of 6.5 to 7.4, while a pH above 7.4 will cause the plants to slowly start to suffer ill effects. The sodium and other salts cause an alkaline pH to develop in a potting mixture.

An important point to remember about using the letters pH in writing or making presentations is the "p" is always lowercase and "H" is always uppercase. Remember, pH is a mathematical measurement. The lowercase "p" indicates a logarithmic scale is being used. In logarithmic scales, for each unit of change (from 1 to 2 or from 2 to 1) there is a ten fold change in the concentration in whatever is being measured.

IMPORTANT RULE ABOUT pH VALUES
From *African Violets: Gifts from Nature*

"Each change of one full unit on the pH scale means a tenfold change in the hydrogen or hydroxyl concentration present in the water solution held in the pore spaces (voids) of the potting mixture.

Example: pH 5.0 is ten times more acid than pH 6.0 and one hundred times [10 x 10] more acid than pH 7.0. Knowing this rule, it is easy to see the pH change from 6.6 to 5.6 [a ten fold increase in acidity] will definitely have an effect on the healthy growth of an African violet.

Question 97 **I have read about the importance of having the proper potting mixture pH and knowing how to test the mixture to determine the pH. But can you tell me how the different pH readings affect my African violets?**

Soil acidity and alkalinity play important roles in the life of an African violet. Many of the problems a plant faces can be traced directly to having the wrong potting mixture pH for healthy growth. The essential plant foods are held tightly in the potting mixture at specific pH readings and at other readings the roots easily absorb the plant food. For maximum availability of the nutrients the ideal pH of a potting mixture should be in the range of 6.5 to 7.0.

The pH of the potting mixture is a life and death matter to many of the beneficial bacteria found in the potting mixture. If these microorganisms are to do their job properly the optimum pH must be maintained in the potting mixture.

Roots may become dehydrated if the pH is too high (alkaline), allowing an excess of salts to accumulate, drawing the moisture from the tender roots.

Question 98 **My African violets are doing well. They blossom all the time and appear to be healthy. I have never concerned myself with the pH of the potting mixture. So why is pH stressed so much when my plants are doing well without my worrying about it?**

Melvin J. Robey

Maybe you are lucky and the pH of your potting mixture is just right for good African violet growth. In all likelihood, you are giving your plants a lot of tender loving care and using excellent growing techniques.

While the plants are doing well, there is the possibility they could perform at a higher level for you if you found the pH was not in the range favored by African violets.. For instance, it is not uncommon for African violet blossoms to lose some of their brilliance when the potting mixture pH changes only a little bit. The serious hobbyists will always make it a point to check the pH of the potting mixture to ensure the best possible performance from their African violet.

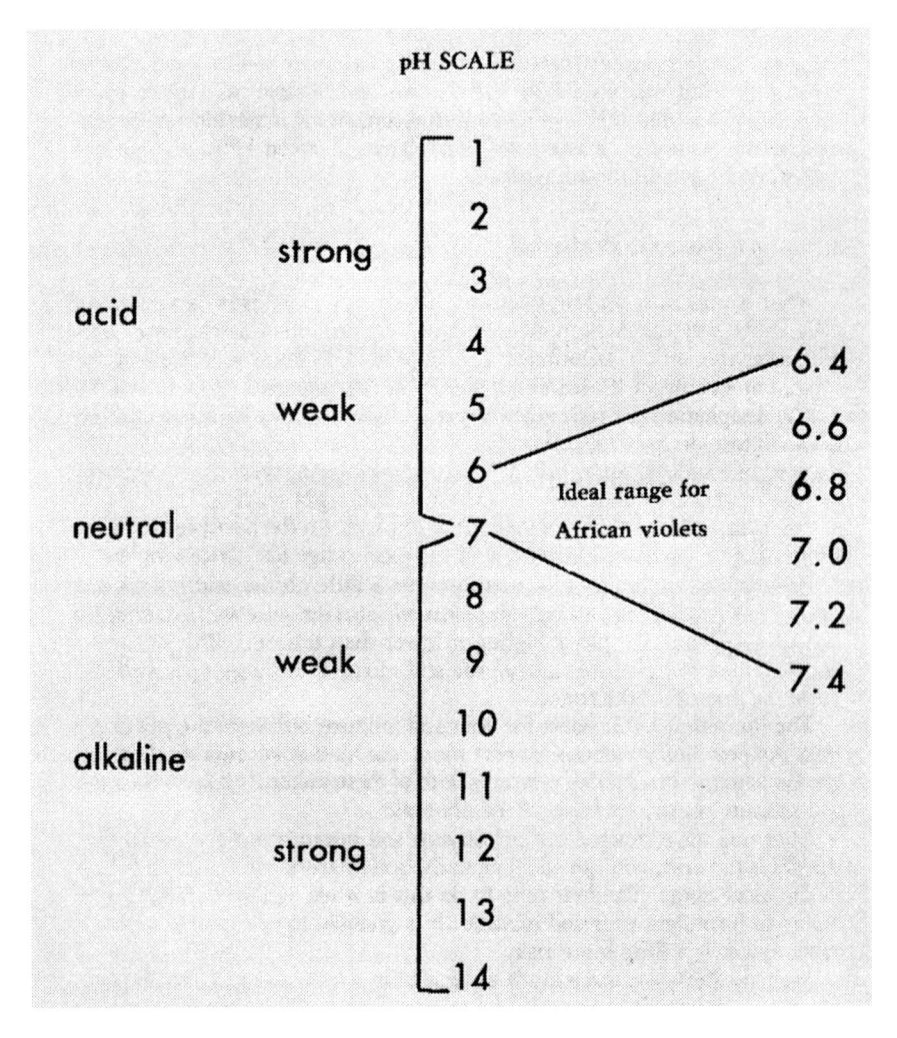

pH SCALE

acid	strong	1, 2, 3, 4
	weak	5, 6
neutral		7
alkaline	weak	8, 9, 10
	strong	11, 12, 13, 14

Ideal range for African violets: 6.4, 6.6, 6.8, 7.0, 7.2, 7.4

From: *African Violets: Queens of the Indoor Gardening Kingdom*

Question 99 I had my potting mixture tested to determine whether it was alkaline or acid. The reading sent to me was 7.4. What should I use to reduce this number to be slightly acid?

Check your local garden centers for products containing sulfur which are specifically formulated to reduce the pH of a potting mixture.

Ferrous sulfate will do the job for you. It can be bought at most pharmacies and is not expensive. An ounce or two will last you a long time. Mix one-quarter teaspoon of the powder into one gallon of water and stir it well. Use this solution to water your plants and the pH reading will slowly move down into the range where healthy African violets thrive.

There is another product available if you know someone in the agriculture profession or a golf course superintendent. Ammonium sulfate (21% nitrogen and 24% sulfur) will also gradually reduce the pH from alkaline into the acid range. A word of caution though, if you continue to use these types of products you will eventually lower the pH too much, creating a new set of problems. You will need to have the potting mixture pH checked again after using the solution for a few weeks.

Question 100 If the pH is so important to the plant where can I buy something for testing the pH of my potting mixture?

Small soil test kits are available at most garden centers. They have a couple of bottles of chemicals you add to the soil or potting mixture. The hydrogen and/or salts in the potting mixture will change the color of the liquid poured onto a small amount of the potting mixture. Then all you have to do is compare the color of the liquid with a special color chart which comes with the kit and you will have the pH of the potting mixture.

Question 101 I know the pH range of 6.5 to 7.4 is ideal to get my plants to growth healthily and produce an abundance of flowers. Can you give me some examples of pH values of everyday products used around my house?

The following table shows several items and the pH at which most of them occur.

pH	Item	pH	Item	pH	Item
1.5	stomach liquid	4.8	sour milk	7.9	sea water
2.3	lemon juice	6.0	fresh milk	9.5	soap
3.8	orange juice	7.0	pure water	12.0	bleach
4.0	tomato juice	7.3	human blood	13.5	oven cleaner

CHAPTER 5

CONTAINERS FOR GROWING BEAUTIFUL AFRICAN VIOLETS

Question 102 **When discussing the diameter of a pot, is the measurement given for the top or bottom of the pot?**

The diameter is measured across the top or the opening of the pot.

Question 103 **Strawberry pots would make an excellent container for growing African violets. Which types of plants would do best in these pots?**

Many cultivars of African violets would do fine when potted in a strawberry pot. The key to being successful is to select plants which grow small and bloom profusely. Trailing African violets would do nicely in these pots. These plants produce an unusually high number of blossoms when given plenty of light. Miniature African violets, because of their compact growth, will also do well in these unique pots. When you first place your African violets in the pot remember it will take three to six weeks before they become as attractive as you are anticipating.

The Supremes, Amazons, and DuPont type plants produce too big of plants and in most cases should not be selected for use.

Question 104 **Does the depth of the pot have any effect on how well a plant will do in it?**

An African violet plant will always do its best when its roots are growing throughout the potting mixture. For this reason, the short, squatty pots would be best for the health of the plant. This allows the roots to easily grow down into the mixture and reduces the chances of the potting mixture turning sour due to remaining wet for too long.

Question 105 **Is it necessary to have a drain hole in a pot?**

African Violets Back to the Basics

The primary reason for having a drain hole in a pot is to allow water an avenue to escape when to much water is added to the top of the potting mixture. Another advantage of having a drain hole is to assist in the leaching of salts, which prevents any build up of salts from occurring in the potting mixture.

If you are careful not to over water then the drain hole is not necessary, although it is a good idea to select a pot with a drain hole whenever possible—just in case you accidentally over water. Also, if you added a layer of charcoal to the bottom of the pot you have a little extra margin of safety from problems that occur due to overwatering.

A drain hole is necessary if you plan on wick or mat watering your plants.

Question 106 **I just tossed out a sick African violet because some kind of wilting disease ruined its appearance. Is it okay to put another plant in the same ceramic pot or should I get rid of the pot too?**

With the cost of ceramic pots I would not toss it into the garbage yet. I also would not recommend potting another African violet in it either until you are sure it is safe for a new plant. Once a disease gets a foothold on a plant there is a good possibility it will cling to the sides of the pot, even after tossing the sick plant out. This is especially true if it is a porous clay pot.

Two steps need to be taken before re-using the pot. First, wash all the potting mixture from inside and outside of the pot. Next, sterilize the pot by placing it in an oven or pressure cooker.

Question 107 **The size pot to use always puzzles me when selecting one for my African violets? Are there any guidelines I can follow to ensure healthy plants?**

I can give you some suggestions on pot sizes but I am not going to guarantee you will always have healthy plants. Many other factors have an effect on the health of your African violets.

I always start a new plant, from a cutting or seed, in a pot with a 2½-inch diameter. This size pot is big enough to satisfy the African violet's needs for the first year of its growth, often even longer. Be sure the roots have completely grown throughout the potting mixture before moving a plant into a larger pot. The next size pot I use is usually 3 to 4 inches in diameter and will be the final home for my African violets. Very seldom will you need to grow an African violet in a pot with a diameter greater than four inches.

Question 108 **Is there any relationship between pot size and flowering?**

There definitely is. If you place an African violet in a pot that is too large it will produce very few flowers for you. These plants flower best when their roots have completely grown throughout the potting mixture. Your best bet is to put your African violets in a small pot, transferring them to slightly larger pots as the roots fill out into all the potting mixture. This way you will have a happy plant producing plenty of blossoms for your enjoyment.

Every pot should have a drain hole to allow excess water to drain from the potting mixture. From *African Violets: Gifts from Nature.*

Question 109 What are some of the advantages and disadvantages of clay pots and plastic pots?

CLAY POTS
Advantages:
1. A variety of sizes from which to choose
2. Matching saucers are available
3. Porosity of pot allows air and water to easily move thorough the pot into the potting mixture
4. A drain hole is always present

Disadvantages:
1. Not as decorative as other types of pots
2. They require frequent wateringz

3. The accumulation of salts on the sides and the rims of the pots mars their appearance
4. Accumulated salts on the rim of pots may cause petiole (stem) rot

PLASTIC POTS
<u>Advantages</u>:
1. A huge selection of decorative pots are available
2. Plastic pots do not weight very much
3. They are easy to clean
4. They require less watering to meet the plants needs
5. A wide variety of colors are available
6. Drain holes are usually present

<u>Disadvantages</u>:
1. There is a tendency of the potting mixtures to become waterlogged
2. The air and moisture are unable to move through the sides of the pot into the potting mixture
3. They are often more expensive

Question 110 **How come there is such a terrible odor when I sterilize my clay pots in the oven?**

If you do not wash all the potting mixture and grime from the pot there will always be a stink when trying to sterilize your pots in the oven. Be sure to do a thorough job because it only takes a little bit of debris in the pot to cause a smelly problem.

Sometimes, even after scrubbing the pots, there is still an odor problem. This is caused by minute particles being trapped in the porous sides of the pots. To solve this problem soak the pots in clean water for a few hours, then place them in the oven. You may want to add ammonia or Clorox to help dislodge material from the pots. If you do this be sure to thoroughly rinse the pots before using them again.

Question 111 **Why do some people soak their clay pots before planting their African violets in them?**

The red clay pots are very porous and are usually very dry when a new plant is placed in them. This often causes a considerable amount of the water to be pulled from the potting mixture into the drier pots. So, until these pots are wetted they rob moisture from the potting mixture, causing it to dry out sooner. To avoid having to water the plants frequently for the first week after planting, some growers pre-soak the pots to eliminate this nuisance. With my plants I have never notice this to be much of a problem and usually do not worry about pre-soaking any pots. It may be tender loving care is a factor here.

POTTING PLANTS

Question 112   **Should I plant my African violets in small pots or large pots?**
You will have healthier, happier plants if you keep them in small pots. African violets do not do well when their roots are set in a pot with lots of extra potting mixture. The plant itself will flower more profusely when it is slightly pot bound. Another good reason for using the smaller pots is they require less space in your plant room or when being displayed in various locations in your home. This will allow you to keep more plants in the limited area you may have available for them.

Question 113   **I have broken my clay pots on several occasions when I have been trying to get plants out of them. Is there an easy way to remove the plants?**
The technique I have used successfully is to push a pencil, eraser end, up through the drain hole. This easily dislodges the potting mixture, allowing the plant to be removed from the pot without damaging the pot. Of course, I am assuming your pots have a drain hole in them. If they do not then try to slip a knife down along the sides of the pot to loosen the potting mixture from the sides of the pot. After this is done a few firm raps on the bottom of the pot with the heal of your hand should cause the plant to slip out of the pot. Whichever you use let the potting mixture dry out a little bit. A wet potting mixture tends to resist sliding out of the pot.

Question 114   **How deep should African violets be planted in a pot?**
I do not know how many African violets I have seen setting so deep in the pot that the first and second rows of leaves are touching the rim. In clay pots when this happens a disaster is not far away. The salt-crusted rim of the pot will damage the leaves touching the rim, eventually causing petiole rot.

When the crown of the plant is below the rim, excessive watering floods to the rim of the pot. This immerses the crown in water, allowing the crown rot fungus (*Pythium*) to attack the plant. A good rule of thumb to follow when potting African violet plants is to fill the potting mixture up to one-quarter of an inch below the pot's rim. This will allow for adequate water retention. Also the crown of the plant will be setting level with or above the rim of the pot which will help prevent it from accidentally becoming wet.

Question 115   **Should the soil be wet or dry when I am removing plants from their pots?**

African Violets Back to the Basics

A plant and its soil ball will slip out of the pot easier if the potting mixture is dry. A wet potting mixture is sticky and tends to grip the sides of the pot, causing some damage to occur to the roots unless you are extremely careful. Do not let the potting mixture become so dry it readily crumbles apart when it is remove from the pot. This will be damaging to the roots.

Use a pencil to gently push a plant from a pot. From *African Violets: Gifts from Nature*

Question 116 I have a plant that has dropped most of the lower leaves and looks awful. What can I do besides throw it away?

A "necky" African violet can be restored to its former self with very little difficulty. Simply remove the plant from the pot, cut off the bottom 1 to 1½ inches of the root mass and set the plant back in the pot. Next fill up around the exposed stalk (neck) with a good, loose potting mixture, bringing the new surface to within a quarter of an inch of the pots rim. Water the plant as usual and in a very short time new roots will begin to develop from the stalk (neck) you buried.

Question 117 After potting my African violets there seems to be a two to four week period where the plants do not produce any new leaves or blossoms. Is this normal for African violets?

Any type of plant will show a certain degree of shock after it has been through a potting session. This condition should not last for very long if the plant was healthy at the time of the potting. To help reduce the shock to the plant's system be sure and handle it as gently as possible. Do not disturb anymore of the root system than is absolutely necessary. After the potting job is completed thoroughly saturate the potting mixture with water, letting the excess drip out the drain hole. Repeat this procedure a second time about four hours later to ensure the roots all have a chance to absorb some water and the entire potting mixture has been wetted.

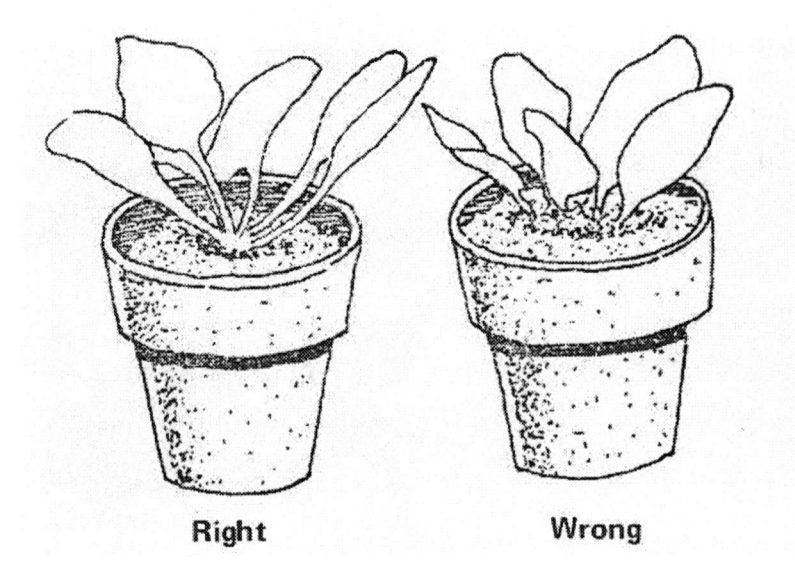

Right   **Wrong**

When potting plants place them in the potting mixture so the crown is barely above the surface of the mixture. Courtesy of West Virginia University

Question 118 After repotting a plant which type of light should it receive—direct or partially filtered light?

Whatever you do, do not place newly potted plants in bright sunlight. Give them about a week to recuperate from being moved. Bright sunlight will cause the water in the potting mixture to quickly evaporate, possible causing root damage. Remember keeping the potting mixture moist is important while the roots grow out into the new potting mixture. Also, direct sunlight may sunburn the leaves.

African Violets Back to the Basics

REPOTTING TECHNIQUES

Question 119 **The tops of my African violets are tipsy and lean to one side in the pot. What can I do to correct this?**

It sounds as if you are dealing with a necky plant. You can remedy this situation by repotting the plant a little deeper in a new pot. Remove the bottom half of the root mass, lightly scrape the stalk where the older leaves are missing. Next place the plant back in the same pot and fill in the pot with fresh potting mixture. Chances are you also have not been giving the plants enough light and they are spindly, with the leaves growing straight up towards the ceiling or leaning towards the direction of the light they are receiving.

Besides being unattractive, a necky plant is more susceptible to disease problems. The plant often becomes wobbly, leaning over onto the rim of the pot, where salts can cause petiole rot to occur. From *African Violets: Gifts from Nature*

Question 120 **Every time I repot my plants I make a big mess. My potting mixture gets all over the leaves, pots, and countertop. Is there a simple way to avoid this?**

No matter how careful you are there are times when the potting mixture is going to spill over the edges of the pot. One technique I have found that works well is to remove the African violet from the old pot, laying the plant aside for a few minutes while using the old pot for a mold. Place this pot in the larger container in which you are potting the African violet and fill in the potting mixture between the two pots. Loosely pack the potting mixture so you can remove the inner pot, leaving a mold opening in the potting mixture the same size as the root mass on the plant your repotting. Slip the African violet into the opening and gently firm up the potting mixture around the root mass.

Question 121 **Is there a handy rule I can use in determining when to repot my plants?**
A general rule of thumb for the correct size of pot for an African violet is—the pot's diameter should be one third of the diameter of the African violet. For example, if you have a nine-inch diameter African violet it should be in a three-inch diameter pot. If it is in a smaller pot then you should consider repotting it. A sure sign of a plant needing to be repotted is when you find the roots growing around the outside of the soil ball.

Question 122 **Whenever I repot my African violets it seems I manage to break off one or two leaves. Can anything be done to avoid this?**
This is a certain way to ruin the looks of some of your favorite plants. The following technique should help you solve this problem. Prior to repotting your plants do not water them for several days. Wait until the leaves and stems have barely begun to wilt. When the cells in these stems start losing their moisture they lose their rigidity (turgor) and become limber. In this stage there is less likelihood of breaking off any leaves while repotting your plants. Be sure to adequately water the plants immediately after repotting them.

Do not forget to take any leaves you do break off and place them in water or a rooting mixture. This way you will turn an accident into several new plants for your future enjoyment.

Question 123 **When repotting plants is there a rule to follow on how much space there should be between the soil ball and the sides of the pots?**
Normally a distance of one-half to three-quarters of an inch should be left between the soil ball and the sides of the pot. This gives you ample room to fill in the new potting mixture without too much trouble. Roots from the soil ball can easily grow into the new potting mixture without any difficulty.

CHAPTER 6

PROPER WATERING TECHNIQUES IMPORTANT

Question 124 If you could pick one problem that causes African violets the most trouble what would it be?

Without any hesitation I believe the number one problem in African violet care is improper watering. It is very difficult to make the instructions clearly understood no matter how much is written or discussed about the correct and best watering methods. The best hope is after gaining a knowledge of a plant's water needs through experimentation and practical experience a proper watering schedule will be set up by the African violet hobbyists.

Question 125 **Everyone knows a plant needs to be watered or it will die. What I want to know is just exactly what are the functions of water in African violets?**

One of the most important roles water plays in an African violet's life is it is one of the basic ingredients needed for photosynthesis. Photosynthesis is the process which produces food (sugars) within the plant.

The cells turbidity (rigidness) depends on the presences of water. When a plant's stems are drooping over the edge of the pot this is due to lack of water being present in the plant's cells. Wilting is easily overcome by watering, restoring the water to the plant's cells. This assumes the wilting was not severe enough to cause the death of any of the cells.

Water is also responsible for transporting the plant's nutrients from the potting mixture up into the plant. Also the loss of water from the leaves as a vapor (transpiration) helps reduce the air temperature around the plant and it increases the humidity as well.

Question 126 **I saw a term used in the gardening section of the Sunday newspaper and was wondering what the writer meant by it. The article** was about watering plants and the term was double potting. Does this refer to having two plants per pot?

The writer was not referring to the number of plants grown in a pot. Double potting is a simple potting technique most often used in office buildings where they have a large number of indoor foliage plants for decorating reception areas and offices.

Usually the reason for double potting an African violet is you have a ceramic or decorative plastic pot which matches your interior decorating theme. For double potting to be most effective the African violet should be in a clay pot with a drain hole. To double pot your African violet you simply need to take the potted plant, place it inside the larger decorative pot, then fill the space between the two pots with sphagnum peat or vermiculite. Be sure the rims of the two pots are level with one another.

When watering you need to pour the water into the pot containing the African violet. You will also need to moisten the sphagnum peat or vermiculite. This will help to keep the clay pot and potting mixture moist for a longer period of time.

Question 127 What is the best way to determine when my plants need to be watered?

There are three simple procedures to use for determining when to water the plants. Two of them are nothing more than keeping an eye on the plants by looking at the color of the potting mixture and the appearance of the plants. A wet potting mixture will usually be a dark color, getting lighter as it dries out. The plant stems will hold the leaves out over the rim of the pot, proudly displaying them if the plant's roots are finding sufficient quantities of water present in the potting mixture. The third procedure is the "touch test." Carefully reach in, touching the potting mixture with your fingertips. It is time to water if it feels dry.

Question 128 A friend and I have been debating about drainage holes in pots. Is it absolutely necessary for a pot to have them?

I have seen African violets doing beautifully in all sorts of containers which did not have a drain hole. The trick to this is to be very careful. Never over water your plants. Also, without a drain hole in the pot, salts will have a tendency to accumulate at the potting mixture surface and will have to be removed, replacing it with fresh potting mixture.

Question 129 I just bought a lovely ceramic container, which perfectly matches my living room décor. The only problem is it does not have a drain hole and I prefer to grow my African violets in a pot that does. What can I do?

I see two solutions to your dilemma. One is to consider using the double potting technique. The other is to take the pot to a commercial glass company and have them cut a drain hole in it. Another risky choice is for you to try drilling a hole through the bottom of the ceramic container. Be careful! Invert the pot and support the inside bottom of the pot on a heavy block of wood. Use a masonry bit and very slowly drill a hole through the bottom of the pot. This technique will usually work. The trick is to go slowly and do not rush the drilling job or you are liable to crack the pot.

Question 130 What can I do to prevent the potting mixture in my pots from turning sour? My decorative ceramic pots do not have a drain hole.

When you use the term sour I am assuming you mean a potting mixture, which has a funny smell to it, is too moist, and algae may be growing on the potting mixture surface. (Sour is also a term used for a potting mixture, which has a low or acid pH.)

Before potting a plant in a container that does not have a drain hole you may wish to try an old technique used by gardeners. Fill the bottom of the pot with charcoal. Charcoal has great absorption ability and helps to keep a potting mixture from becoming waterlogged. You can buy gardening charcoal at almost any garden center.

Be careful not to over water your plants. Apply the water slowly, stopping when the potting mixture is not absorbing anymore. You do not want to have a puddle of water standing in the pot when you have finished watering.

Question 131 Charcoal briquettes used for barbecuing seem to readily absorb the starter fluid used to light a fire. Would it be okay to crush these up and use them in the bottom of a pot?

While these briquettes do have a terrific absorption capacity you should not use them in a pot where you are going to grow any kind of plant. These briquettes have been treated with a petroleum product to ensure they heat up for cooking. This material will move out of the briquettes and into the potting mixture, killing the tender roots of the African violet plants.

WAYS TO WATER PLANTS

Question 132 Do I need to worry about whether I top water or bottom water my African violets?

You do not need to worry about which method you use so long as you understand the pros and cons of each of the watering techniques. Either way is okay. Once you have settled on one, set up a good watering program for healthy, vigorously flowering African violets.

Question 133 **I was told to only water my plants from the bottom. What do you think of this advice? As a beginner I was planning on water from the top but now I do not know what to do.**

Why is it everyone wants a beginner to water their plants from the bottom? This is almost an automatic response to any new African violet fan's question about how to water properly. It makes absolutely no difference to an African violet plant whether you top or bottom water.

What everyone is concerned about is if the beginner waters from the top they may get the crown wet (causing crown rot), drip water on the leaves (often causing ugly blotches), or under watering (which lets the soluble salts accumulate on the potting mixture surface). If you only have a few plants top watering is easy and quick. Wick watering or using mats is an option to save time when there are a lot of plants involved.

When top watering pour the water directly onto the surface of the potting mixture, never onto the center of the plant or leaves. From *African Violets: Gifts from Nature*

Question 134 **Summer is here at last and with it arrives a long awaited vacation. For six months I have been planning this vacation but now I am worried about my African violets. What can I do to be sure they will be okay when I return in two weeks?**

If I were you I would use the wick method of watering while on vacation. Try to anticipate how much water the plants will need while you are gone and have a water reservoir big enough to last the plants. Put your plants on a wick watering schedule two or three weeks before you leave on vacation. This way you will know the wicks are doing their job, which will allow you to enjoy your well-deserved vacation.

It is always a good idea to have a friend check on your plants two or three times while you are gone.

Wick method of watering African violets.
Courtesy of Purdue University

Question 135 **Can you explain how to use wicks and where to find them?**

Special wicks are available at garden centers or you can make your own out of heavy thread, yarn, carpenter twine, nylon cord, or even old nylon stockings. For pots with plants in them already, push the wicks up through the drain hole, being careful not to damage to many of the plant's roots. The wick must come into good contact with the potting mixture. Leave approximately two inches of the wick hanging out the bottom of the pot. For new pots fill in the potting mixture around the wick sticking up through the drain hole.

Next fill a tray with water and arrange your pots so the wick, which is hanging out of the bottom, comes directly in contact with the water. The wick will draw the moisture up into the pot as the plant uses the water from the potting mixture. Several plants can have their wicks in the same watering tray. Now all you have to do is occasionally fill the trays. Always watch your plants for any signs of wilting just in case a wick is not functioning properly.

Question 136 **Are there any advantages to "wick watering" African violets?**

Besides saving a lot of time there are some definite benefits plants can derive from this technique of watering. Often the African violets will respond by growing much larger and by having better color to their foliage. These sturdy, healthy plants are most likely responding to an even supply of water. Adding plant food to the water will also enhance the development of the leaves and flowers.

Question 137 **Can you explain to me exactly how mat watering works?**

Mat watering is a method of bottom watering. It is also a popular way to water when a person has a lot of African violets in one location.

The potted plants are set on a water-absorbing mat. The pot must have a drain hole for the water to be pulled (capillary action) up into the pot. The mat and potting mixture must come into contact with each other. The water moves up into the potting mixture at a slow and constant rate. Clay pots work best when using this watering technique. The pots and potting mixture absorb the water. This gradual, consistent water supply generally produces healthier plants.

Question 138 **What are the disadvantages of mat watering?**

Since the mats are constantly wet there is an increased chance of disease and insect problems. Both types of pest will easily spread to all your plants if proper attention is not given to these potential problems.

A good way to control these pests is to lightly sprinkle a pesticide on the mat. Physan 20 is one pesticide that will control algae on the mats.

WATER TEMPERATURE CRITICAL

Question 139 **Will flowering of my favorite African violet be affected in anyway if I do not use tepid water?**

African violets definitely do not like cold water. If the water is not room temperature your plants may become very stubborn, refusing to produce those lovely blossoms you enjoy. Let the water you use set for twenty-four hours in an open container in the same room your African violets are displayed. This allows the water to reach the correct temperature for use in watering your plants. If there is any chlorine in the water it will evaporate during this period.

Mat watering is one of the most popular ways to water African violets. The water from the moist mat moves up into the potting mixture (indicated by the arrows). The constant, even supply of water promotes health6y growing plants.

Question 140 **My African violets have quit flowering and I cannot figure out why. Could the water I am using have any effect on whether the plants will or will not flower?**

If you are using water that is too cold it could force your African violets to stop producing blossoms for you. The roots of your plants are very temperature sensitive and cold water shocks them, giving the rest of the plant notice of the problem. This triggers a plant's defense mechanisms and shuts down the formation of any new flower buds. However, I would not consider this to be the problem until you had eliminated a few others. Is the temperature around the plants too hot or too cold? Are the plants receiving enough light? Are you over fertilizing with nitrogen? Is there too little humidity around the plants? Check out all these questions, along with the water temperature and you should find a solution to why your plants quit flowering.

WATER QUALITY IMPORTANT

Question 141 **Does it matter if I use tap water when watering my African violets? I have talked to several people about this and have received conflicting recommendations.**

This question is subject to as much controversy as whether you should top water or bottom water African violets.

You will always receive a wide array of answers to both questions. But, to answer your specific question on whether tap water is okay to use I think your own experience will eventually provide the best answer. Some of the things you will need to take into consideration are: (1) How hard is the water? By this I mean is it high in salts, especially sodium. (2) Is it chlorinated? (3) Do you have a soft water conditioner installed in your home? (4) Do you top water or bottom water your plants?

Let's take a brief look at each of these four questions to see how they affect your use of tap water. Hard water contains numerous salts, which if allowed to build up in the potting mixture could become harmful to the plants. Your local water company can tell you if your tap water is to salty for healthy plant development. Chlorinated water indirectly affects the health of your African violets by killing the microscopic organisms found in the potting mixture. These organisms are responsible for releasing the plant nutrients into the water so the roots can absorb them. If you have a soft water conditioner in your home the tap water will have a lot of sodium in it. Sodium build up in the potting mixture can be detrimental to the plants health. If you top water all the time or only occasionally, letting the water drip out the drain hole will wash many of the accumulated salts out of the potting mixture. This will help prevent a salt build up from occurring in your potting mixture.

Question 142 **Our water is heavily chlorinated. What can I do to make this water safe for watering my African violets?**

There is a very easy solution to your problem. Simply fill up jars or some other types of containers with the water then let them sit for twenty-four hours before using the water. Do not cap the containers or put lids on them. The chlorine readily evaporates from the water, escaping into the air as a harmless gas.

Question 143 **Will it damage my African violets to water them occasionally with tap water that is chlorinated?**

No, so long as you are not using this water every day. Small amounts of chlorine will not adversely affect the bacteria in the potting mixture, nor harm you African violets.

Question 144 **If the water from the tap is high in salt due to the water softener where could I obtain good water for my plants?**

There are several options open to you. In the warm months I have used the water the dehumidifier removes from the air in my home. I have even read where some gardeners use snow but it takes a lot of melted snow to supply the necessary water for several African violets. This probably is not the best idea, since snow is often highly contaminated. An old-time favorite of many African violet hobbyists is to collect rainwater. Again, this water is often contaminated. If you have a tap that is hooked up to your water supply before it goes through the water softener then this water is probably okay. If you use this hard water you will have to leach some of the salts out of the potting mixture to prevent a salt accumulation at the surface of the potting mixture

As a last resort you can buy distilled water in jugs from the grocery stores.

WATERING PROBLEMS

Question 145 **I prefer watering my plants by setting them in a pan of water. Does it matter how long I leave the pots in the water?**

Yes. African violet roots are very sensitive to waterlogged potting mixtures. If you let this condition occur and allow it to last too long you may severely damage your plants. Do not leave the pots sitting in the pan of water for more than 30 to 40 minutes, then let the excess water drain from the potting mixture. This should prevent your African violets from suffering any setbacks due to the way you are watering them.

Question 146 I have been told when I am top watering I should be careful not to get any water on the crown of the plant. Is this true and if so, why?

Whoever you have been talking with about watering African violets has given you some excellent advice. Never allow water to get on the crown of your plants. If you do the chances are you will see your plants suddenly start to become very sick. The leaves will droop over the edge of the pots as if you have not watered them for days. When this happens you can bet the crown rot fungus is at work on your plants.

When you accidentally spill water on the crown take a piece of soft tissue paper and carefully soak up the water until the crown is once again dry.

Question 147 Why is it necessary to avoid getting water on the leaves of my plants? The few times I have spilled water on the leaves nothing has happened.

There are several reasons why spilling water on the leaves of African violets can harm the plants sooner or later. If you continue getting water on the leaves you can be sure of seeing some problems showing up on your plants.

Often when the water evaporates off the leaf's surface a whitish mark is deposited on the leaf. This mark is due to the salts present in the water. The appearance of an attractive plant can easily be ruined under these circumstances. It is almost impossible to remove the whitish salt marks left on a leaf.

Another problem that is very likely to occur is leaf scorch (sun burned). This happens whenever water droplets are allowed to stand on the leaf when it is receiving full or partial sunlight. The water tends to magnify the sun's rays, causing them to burn or scorch the leaf surface. This kills the plant's cells and causes a brownish dead spot to mar the leaf surface.

If the water you are using is too hot or cold it can also damage the leaf and kill the plant tissue.

Question 148 I forgot to water one of my plants and the potting mixture dried up and shrunk away from the sides of the pot. When I water all of the it runs down the sides of the pot and out the bottom, without thoroughly wetting the dried potting mixture. How should have I rewetted the potting mixture?

A simple procedure to use is to fill a pan with water and set the pot, with the dried potting mixture, into the water. The water level should come up to within ½ inch of the pots rim. This allows the water to move up from the bottom and slowly rewet all the potting mixture. After approximately 30 minutes remove the pot from the pan and let the excess water drain out. In about two hours water the plant again, from the top, letting some water drip out the drain hole. This will complete the rewetting process of your potting mixture.

Another technique to use is to place ice cubes on the potting mixture. The ice melts slowly, allowing all the water to be absorbed by the potting mixture.

Be careful in the future or you may lose too many roots when the potting mixture dries out, causing the African violet plant's growth to be severely retarded for several weeks.

Question 149   **My collection of African violets is up to twenty-eight and I have them scattered in every room of my house. My problem is this: I like to let a little water drip out the bottom when I water but it takes forever to carry each plant to the sink. What can I do?**

One of the most time consuming jobs when caring for African violets is watering them, especially if you like to top water. To save time and still let a little water drip out the drain hole I have used the following technique successfully. I carry a quart jar with me and set each pot down into this jar so the pot's are supported on the jars rim. Now when the water drips from the drain hole of my potted African violet it is collected in the jar below. When I am through watering all my plants I pour the excess water from the quart jar down the kitchen sink.

Question 150   **Is it okay to mix plant food in with the water I am using on my African violet?**

Yes. Simple dissolve the fertilizer in the water. Most fertilizers you buy from the houseplant section of the garden centers will have instructions for you to follow. Do not spill any of the fertilizer solution on the leaves as it may cause a fertilizer burn, which will cause dead spots on the leaves.

Question 151   **Do my plants use less water during the cooler winter months? It seems like I do not have to water them as much during the short days.**

You have made an excellent observation which eludes many indoor gardeners. With the shorter winter days comes the fact that the sun's intensity has been greatly reduced. Because of this the plant's growth has slowed down and it needs less water. The further north you live the more noticeable this is in the wintertime. As the warmer summer days approach you will see this trend change gradually and additional water will be required by your African violets.

CHAPTER 7

THOSE UGLY PESTS

INSECTS, DISEASES, & OTHER UNSIGHTLY PROBLEMS

Question 152 There has been so much said about how delicate the African violet plant is I am almost afraid to try my hand growing them. One of my concerns is how diseases and insects bother them. Am I worried over nothing?

It is time to bury the myth about the delicate nature of the African violet plant. African violets will take as much abuse as any other indoor plant. While they may refuse to flower on occasion, you do not have to pamper them like a baby to keep them happy. These plants are susceptible to a few diseases and insects but I certainly would not let this stop you or anyone else from growing them.

Follow good growing practices and chances are excellent you will have very little trouble with these lovely plants. However, prepare yourself so you can identify a disease or insect problem and be able to take the appropriate action whenever you first notice a problem developing with your plants.

Question 153 Will too much plant food cause any problems for my plants?

If you feed an African violet too much fertilizer high in nitrogen you can cause the plant to become more susceptible to disease attacks. Nitrogen causes rapid growth of the plant and the young cell tissue is very tender. Such plant tissue is not able to ward off disease organisms, thus making it easier for a fungus, bacteria, or virus to infect the plant tissue.

Question 154 **I was told plants suffering from the lack of plant food and salt damage are considered to have a disease. I always thought a fungus or some sort of living creature caused a disease. Which is true?**

Plant scientists have divided plant diseases into two classifications: physiological and biological. A few of the physiological diseases caused by improper care of the plants are: too little or too much light, over or under watering, too much or too little plant food, and placing plants in drafts. The biological diseases are caused by: fungi, bacteria, viruses, and nematodes.

More African violets die due to the physiological diseases than for any other reason. So if you want to have your favorite African violets around, cheering up your home for a long time, pay attention to their daily needs—especially your watering habits.

Question 155 **Could you provide me with a list of the chemicals for getting rid of any insect or disease killers?**

Due to the various laws the Federal and State governments have passed on the use of pest killers it is usually best to ask your local County Extension Agent this question. Another good place to look for information on pest killers is in the African Violet Society of America's magazine articles and in the advertisements. Whatever you use, be sure to read the label and learn how a pesticide should be applied. A mistake could be fatal to your African violets and you!

Always carefully read the label directions on any pesticide you are planning to use. Be sure to follow the directions and do not store the container where small children or your pets can get into them.

<u>Protect Your Most Precious Love Ones!</u>

Approximately 50% of all household poisonings [which includes pesticides] happen to children 10 years old or younger. Within this age group 95% of the deaths occur to the children 5 years old or younger.

Melvin J. Robey

WHAT

IS

THIS

5

YEAR

OLD

THINKING?

Courtesy of Purdue University

Partial List of Insecticides for Use on African Violets*

Aphids	Orthene, Ficam, Talstar, Dursban, Di-syston, Thiodan, Dibrom, and Malathion
Broad Mites	Talstar, Trithion, Dursban, Kelthane, and Thiodan
Cyclamen Mite	Orthene, Trithion, Dursban, Kelthane, and Thiodan
Earwigs	Sevin and Baygon
Foliar Mealybugs	Orthene, Ficam, Talstar, Trithion, Dursban, Cygon, Thiodan, and Malathion
Fungus Gnats	Malathion
Scales	Orthene, Ficam, Sevin, Cygon, Di-syston, and Thiodan
Soil Mealybugs	Kelthane, Orthene, Ficam, Talstar, Trithion, Dursban, Thiodan, and Malathion
Spider Mites	Talstar, Sevin, Trithion, Kelthane, Di-syston and Thiodan
Thrips	Cygon, Dursban, Di-system, Ficam, Orthene, and Sevin

*Compiled from Dr. C.L. Cole's table published in the *African Violet Magazine*, November/December 1994, page 19.

Question 156 **I worry about using bug killers around the house but my African violets are in need of some help. Bugs have literally taken over. Before using a bug killer in my home what kinds of things do I need to be aware of?**

You should know there is not a single recorded death of a human being from any pesticide (bug killer), which was used according to the labeled directions on the container. Therefore, the first rule you need to be aware of is: ALWAYS READ THE LABEL AND CAREFULLY FOLLOW THE DIRECTIONS.

When the bug killer (insecticide) is not being used it should be placed in a locked cabinet where small children cannot reach it. Children under the age of five have the highest fatality rate from household poisons and pesticides.

Question 157 **What is the purpose of keeping new African violets, just brought into the house, separated from the rest of my collection?**

Many beautiful collections of healthy African violets have been wiped out because enthusiastic hobbyists introduced a disease and/or bug-infested plant into a collection of plants already growing in their homes. For this reason a two-month quarantine period should be enforced on all new plants—regardless of the source. It would not hurt to spray an insecticide on the new plants two or three times during this period. After the quarantine period is over if you have not seen any insects or disease problems you can move the new plants in with the others.

DISEASES ARE BOTHERSOME

Question 158 **What are some of the different diseases I need to worry about? What causes them? And what are the symptoms they cause?**

You must be concerned with airborne and soilborne diseases when growing African violets. Airborne diseases, Gray mold (*Botrytis* Mold) and powdery mildew, are easily spotted. Both cause a fuzzy-like growth to form on the infected parts of the plant. If this fuzzy growth (actually the fungus plant itself) is white, your plants are infected with powdery mildew. A straw colored, fuzzy growth indicates gray mold is the culprit. High humidity allows both diseases to get a firm foothold on your African violets.

Soilborne diseases can be divided into two groups: crown rot and root rot. Both are caused either by using potting mixtures, which have not been sterilized, or keeping the potting mixture to wet by overwatering. Plant symptoms displayed when infected with these diseases are: decaying roots, decaying crowns, and wilting leaves. When watering, crown rot may also be caused when water is poured directly onto the center of the plant.

Question 159 **Mildew is ruining the appearance of my favorite African violets. What is causing this problem?**

Two different fungi, discussed in the previous question's answer, may be the culprits. These organisms will attack African violets when the humidity is very high around your plants. You have to be doing a good job of raising the humidity around your plants for these fungi to be bothering them. Forty percent relative humidity is sufficient for good plant growth. If you have it any higher then diseases usually become a problem.\

Question 160 **To what is the term "bud blast" referring?**

Whenever you have a plant which drops its flower buds before they open you have bud blast. It is just another way of saying the flower buds are prematurely dropping off the plant. This may or may not be caused by a fungus.

Question 161 **Why are the flower buds on my African violet dropping off before they open? This is very discouraging!**

I can understand your being unhappy over the loss of what would become gorgeous blossoms. Several factors could cause the buds to fall off before opening. A fungus, *Botrytis* Gray Mold, is a strong possibility if you have had the humidity too high around the plants. Usually you will find a straw-colored, fuzzy growth on the buds if this disease is the problem.

Question 162 **Why shouldn't my African violets be crowded together under the artificial lights I have set up? I want as many of these lovely plants around my home as possible but was warned against crowded conditions. However, no reason was given.**

When you crowd too many plants into a small area the air around the plants can become stale. If air circulation is poor among the plants the humidity may become too high. This provides the ideal environment for disease development. If this occurs you may lose all your plants. Avoid over crowded conditions or you may have very few flowering African violets to enjoy.

PHYSIOLOGICAL STRESSES HARD ON PLANTS

Question 163 **I have heard of a "red disease." What is it?**

That's a good question. No one knows for sure what it is. Several plant disease experts have studied African violets displaying the red disease symptom but have not come up with an answer. Insects do not seem to be the culprit, nor does a fungus look to be a likely candidate. Viruses are being considered as suspects. It has been speculated the problem is physiological, such as too much or too little plant food and improper lighting.

Question 164 **What are the symptoms an African violet displays when it has "red disease"?**

The underneath portion of the leaves become very red. New developing growth is stunted with stems also being red. Usually the stems are very short and the leaf may appear to be lacking a stem. This causes the center of the plant to become very compacted (tight). Blossoms will continue to burst forth, sometimes in more abundance than you would normally expect. Old leaves will curl up and their stems become very rigid and brittle. This disease does not kill the plant but after a period of time the plant's appearance is generally ruined, as the foliage is dwarfed or malformed.

Question 165 **Will a leaf cutting taken from a plant, which has the red disease, be free of the problem?**

No. Once a plant is infected the sickness is carried by all leaf cuttings. Do not waste your time with these sick plants, rather spend it raising healthy African violets for your collection. Since this is the case, the speculation that "red disease" is caused by a physiological problem is not a very strong possibility. If it was a physiological problem, as soon as you corrected it, the new growth from the plant would be normal.

Question 166 **I am preparing to paint the room where I keep all my African violets. Is it necessary to remove them from the room?**

It will depend on the type of paint you are using. Usually the water based paints will not release any fumes which will damage your plants. If you are using an enamel paint you should consider removing the plants from the room. The fumes released from enamel-based paints can be toxic to an African violet. Even if you have the room well ventilated I would not take any chances. If you leave the plants in the room remember to cover them to prevent paint splotches from marring their appearance.

Question 167 **Just exactly how does the salt on the rim of the pot cause the stems to rot?**

Salts accumulate on the rim of the pot in a very concentrated form. When the stem (petiole) is in contact with the salt on the rim it only takes a small amount of moisture to dissolve these salts, setting the stage for petiole rot, also called efflorescence disease.

What happens, in a rapid sequence, is the concentrated salts weaken the plant's cells to a point where disease organisms (bacteria and fungi) can enter the stem's cell tissues. These organisms work quickly and in a very short time all the cells in the vicinity of where the stem touched the rim are dead and have started rotting. This cuts off the water supply to the leaf, causing it to become limp and then it dies. Snip this leaf off before it dies. If the stem on the leaf is long enough (at least 1 inch) then it can be used as a cutting. Be sure to cut off the rotting tissue first. This will turn a disaster into several new plants for your continued enjoyment.

Question 168 **Help! My favorite African violet is sick. It was in perfect health when I moved it into the kitchen. Any idea what has happened to it?**

A number of things could have caused the sudden change in the appearance of your plant. If you have a natural gas range in the kitchen then this very likely is the problem. African violets are extremely sensitive to gas fumes. Move the plant away from the range and hopefully your favorite African violet will recover. At the same time take a leaf cutting to ensure you will still have the plant in your collection.

Another possibility is by moving the plant to a new location you have made a major change in the environment where it is now growing. This often adversely affects the plants until they adapt to a new location.

Question 169 **What is causing the small, circular dead spots on the leaves of my plants?**

My first thought is you are using too cold of water when watering your plants. If this water is allowed to drip on the leaf surface a brown spot will develop. Another possibility is the water droplets on the leaves will act as a magnifying lens if the plant is in direct sunlight. Magnified sun rays will burn the plant's cells, killing the cells, and leaving a dead spot the size of the water droplets.

WATCH OUT FOR THOSE BUGS

Question 170 **What are some of the different insect pests that attack African violets?**

An army of invaders could include any of the following pests: cyclamen mites, broad mites, red spider mites, aphids, thrips, springtails, mealybugs, and scales. These are the primary insect problems to watch for.

Question 171 **How is the best way to make sure there are not any pests lurking in the soil mixture in which I plant my African violets?**

Sterilization of the potting mixture will rid it of those unwanted pests. There are three different methods you can use: steam sterilization, heat sterilization, and chemical sterilization. (See Q&A #86)

Question 172 **Does it hurt to dip cuttings in an insect killing solution before placing them in a glass of water to root?**

This is an excellent way to ensure new plants are not going to be infested with bugs, especially the pesky cyclamen mite. Absolutely no damage will be done to a cutting immersed in the solution so long as you are following the labeled directions and the chemical is safe for use on African violet plants. Reading the label will tell you if the chemical can be safely used for insect control on African violets.

Question 173 **About a month ago I brought some potted geraniums in from my outside garden for a centerpiece on my dining table. The African violets I used in the arrangement were soon infested with aphids. I have never had a problem like this with my African violets and suspect the bugs came from the geraniums. What do you think?**

If you are positive the African violets were bug free before the geraniums were brought in from the outside then your suspicions are most likely correct. It is not unusual for insects to get a free ride into a home this way. The next time you plan on using outdoor plants from the garden in your home plan ahead to be able to isolate them for as long as possible and spray them for

Melvin J. Robey

bugs. You could also keep your Africans violets in another room and avoid integrating them into your flower arrangements where outdoor plants are being used.

Question 174 **I do not want to use any kind of chemical killers in my home but I am having a problem with insects. What should I do?**

Since you do not want to use any of the insect killers you will have to rely upon some alternative methods of getting rid of your bugs.

Try washing them off under a stream of warm water, being careful not to get the crown of the plant wet. Another simple technique that is effective is to dip a Q-Tip into rubbing alcohol and touch the insects with the saturated cotton. This will kill the insects. If, after trying this you still have an insect problem you have other choices available to you. One option is to toss the plants out before the insects spread to all your African violets or select an aerosol can of insect spray especially formulated for use on African violets. You stated you did not want to do this but every once in awhile a situation comes along in which extra ordinary steps are needed to solve a particular problem. Another solution is to take your plants outdoors and spray them with a pest killer. Let them set for a little while and then bring them back into the house. If you do this be sure to isolate them from your other plants until you are positive some enterprising bug did not hop on the plants for a free ride into your home.

Question 175 **It looks like I have streaks of pollen on the flower petals. What is causing this?**

Sounds like you have a thrips problem. These tiny insects bore into the sides of the pollen sacs (anthers), allowing the pollen grains to escape and collect on the nearby flower petals. Use a magnifying glass to look for the holes in the anthers (two yellow structures found in the center of the flower). If you find any this will confirm the presences of thrips.

Question 176 **When I am finally convinced my African violets have a virus disease what should I do?**

The one and only solution to a virus infection is to toss the plant in the garbage. If you do not there is an excellent chance the virus will spread to other plants in your home. There is no cure for a virus disease.

Do not even considering taking a leaf cutting, thinking you can start new plants which will be free of the virus. The viruses spread throughout every part of the plant and the new plantlets coming from the leaf cutting will also be infected.

African Violets Back to the Basics

Question 177 **The leaves in the center of my plant are all malformed, sort of knotted up and it looks like the leaves may be hairier than normal. What is happening?**

A combination of those two symptoms makes me suspect an insect is busily attacking your plant. They are too small to see with the naked eye but the plant is showing you what the problem is. Take a close look at the leaf, where they are connected to the stem, and see if at this location the cells are turning yellow. The cyclamen mite likes to feed on this part of the plant and a yellow discoloration, along with what you have described, confirms a cyclamen mite problem.

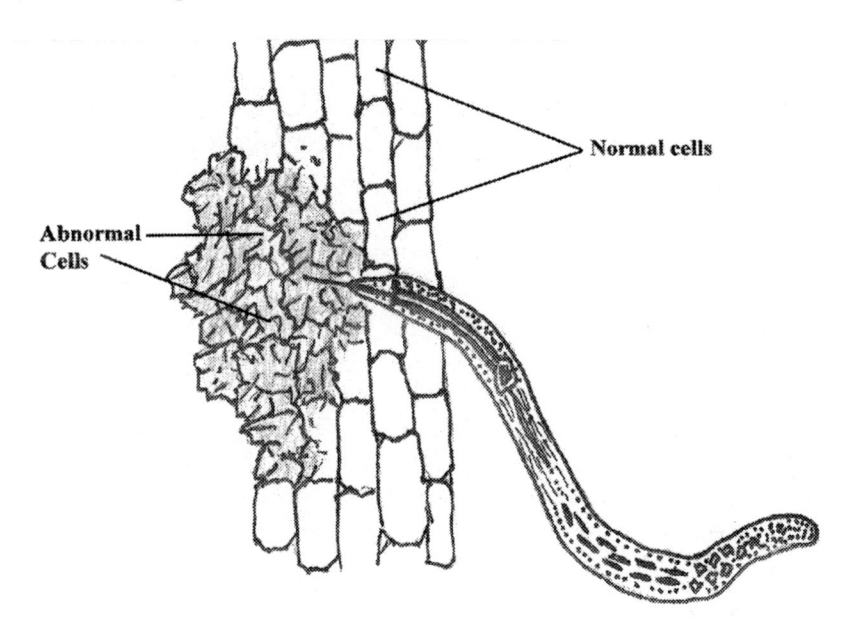

A diagrammatic sketch of a foliar nematode. Notice the shriveled cells where the nematode's stylet has sucked all the plant juices from them. From *African Violets: Gifts from Nature*

Question 178 **Nematodes. What are they?**

Nematodes are microscopic, eel-like creatures capable of causing untold injury to African violets. They attack both the roots and the foliage of the plants and are extremely difficult to detect. Chances are very good that you will never have a nematode problem. The best technique for controlling them is to sterilize the potting mixture prior to using it.

CHAPTER 8

PROPAGATION IS EASY

Question 179 **I would like to increase my collection of African violets by doing my own propagating. What are the different techniques I can use on these delicate plants?**

Basically four different propagating methods are available from which you can choose.

Leaf cuttings

With a sharp knife remove a leaf along with 1½ to 2 inches of stem. Place the stem, cut at an angle, in either water or a potting mixture, leaving the leaf exposed. Roots and new plantlets will develop from this leaf.

Division

This technique is used when a plant has more than one crown with a single root mass. When a plant becomes too large it can be reduced in size by cutting the root mass and crowns into new plants. Or remove one of the crowns and place it in a rooting mixture.

Separation

Separation is used when two or more plants are growing together each with its own root system. The plants are gently separated and repotted into individual pots. This situation occurs frequently when a hobbyists is growing new plants from seeds.

Seeding

Placing seeds in a specially prepared potting mixture and keeping the seeds moist is a good way to add several new plants to your collection.

Question 180 **I have some leaves rooting from a patented African violet. I read where this is illegal. Am I breaking a law?**

It depends on your plans for the new plants. If they are for your own personal enjoyment and to increase the number of African violets you have then you are not in violation of any law. Should you sell the new plants then you are breaking a law and could get into trouble. It is unlikely you would have a problem so long as it is only a very small number of plants involved. My advice is to respect the patent laws and only propagate these plants for your own personal enjoyment. You must obtain a license and pay a fee to propagate patented African violets for resale

Question 181 *A group at the garden club was talking about something called asexual propagation and different ways African violets could be reproduced this way. I did not want to ask them what they meant. Could you tell me?*

The definition of asexual propagation is the reproduction of new plants without the union of male and female germ cells. Leaf cuttings are the best example of this when discussing African violets. A single leaf placed in water or a rooting mixture sends up new plants from the base of the stem. With very few exceptions these plants will be identical to the parent plant from which the leaf was removed.

The opposite of asexual is sexual propagation where each parent plant contributes a germ cell. The fusion of the germ cells in the ovary of one of the plants produces the seed that gives rise to a new generation of plants. These seeds will carry the genetic information from their parents, but they may or may not look like the parent plants. This will depend entirely upon what genes the plants inherited from each of the parents.

Question 182 *Someone told me I had a "sporting" African violet. Is this a special variety, a disease, or what?*

Occasionally a leaf cutting, when rooted, will develop new plants, which are not exactly like the original plant. When this happens the new plants are called sports or more correctly mutants. Many of the new varieties of African violets have been developed this way. An example of this is 'Happy Harold,' an old African violet cultivar, with variegated leaves. The original plant had leaves that were all green and one of these leaves produced a sport with white and green leafed foliage. Similarly, the double blossoms are mutants from the standard blossoms.

Question 183 *What will happen if I cut the stem off and try to root only the leaf?*

Leaf rooting will work, but the chances of success are not as great as leaving a stem on the leaf. A sport or a mutant is liable to develop when using only the leaf. If you want new plants identical to their parent I would not recommend using this technique.

Question 184 **My friend showed me his collection of African violets that had blossoms looking like pinwheels (red stripes down the center of each petal). He called them chimera African violets. What does the word chimera mean?**

A normal African violet has one set of chromosomes in each cell. A set consists of one chromosome from the male donor (stamen) and another from the female acceptor (pistil).

The chimera African violets have some cells, which are genetically different. This means the set of chromosomes in individual cells are not identical with the other cells in the plant. This makes it impossible for these plants to produce seed which will grow into plants with the pinwheel or striped blossoms.

Question 185 **When I try to use leaf cuttings to propagate my African violets, which has pinwheel blossoms, all the new plants produce solid colored blossoms. Why?**

This is not unusual, in fact, it is normal. Plants producing pinwheel or striped blossoms are called chimera African violets. The new plants, which originate from a leaf cutting of a chimera African violet, will always develop solid colored blossoms. To be successful propagating these plants remove any suckers (side-shoots) and root them. Mature plants from these suckers will produce flowers identical to those of the parent plant.

You may also try taking a flower stalk from one of these plants and place it in a rooting mixture. Keep in mind the success rate using this technique is much lower than selecting a sucker.

Question 186 **How long must I wait to determine if a "sucker" is forming and not a flower stalk?**

Do not snip off any new growth from the base of the plant until you are sure what it is. If you are to quick you will end up removing more flower stalks than suckers. Watch the development of the new growth carefully. If you see two small leaves forming do not automatically assume it is a sucker starting to develop. Occasionally a flower stalk will have two very small appendage-like structures, which appear to be leaves. Wait until four distinct leaves can be seen then you can be certain you have a sucker forming. Also by waiting this long you can root the sucker, giving you another African violet for your collection. Suckers are also referred to as side shoots.

The author roots most suckers in pure vermiculite. This sucker is ready for transplanting into a regular potting mixture of peat, perlite, and vermiculite.
From *African Violets: Gifts from Nature*

Question 187 **Will the length of the stem left on a leaf cutting have any effect on whether the new plantlets will be identical to the parent plant?**

Your chances of a sport developing are greatest if you cut the stem off and try rooting the leaf only. To avoid this possibility, always leave 1½ to 2 inches of stem attached to the leaf cutting. This will increase your chances of producing identical plants from a cutting.

Question 188 **I would like to start some leaf cuttings from my favorite African violet. Could you tell me how long it will take for the roots to develop? When will the new plants begin to flower?**

Healthy, young leaves will begin sprouting new roots in approximately four to six weeks. This will vary according to the African violets you have and the various external conditions (temperature, light, air circulation) around the plant. It is not unusual for months to pass before the first signs of new roots can be seen.

Blossoms on the new plants usually begin to develop in four to six months after the new plants (6 to 8 leaves) have become established in a 2½ inch pot.

Question 189   I have a leaf that refuses to root. It has been in the potting mixture for two months and still looks healthy. Should I give up or wait a little bit longer?

Sometimes a leaf cutting will go for months, looking healthy in the potting mixture and never produce any new roots or plantlets. When you selected the leaf for your cutting what part of the African violet did you snip it from? If you took one from the very center or the outer lower row of leaves the chances are this is the problem. The very young and very old leaves have a difficult time producing roots regardless of how long you wait.

Question 190   A friend asked for a start from my favorite African violet. Does it make any difference where I snip it off the plant?

It certainly does. You first must give some consideration to how the missing leaf will affect the appearance of your plant. I would suggest removing any "suckers" that develop and root them to give away whenever someone asks you for a start from your plants. However, if you do not mind snipping leaves from your plants then choose one that is in the second or third row of leaves from the bottom. An old leaf (lowest and outer most row) and a very young leaf (center of the plant) will not develop roots easily. A mature leaf from the second or third row will root and send up new plants to the satisfaction of its owner.

Once the leaf has developed healthy roots in this glass of water, move the plant into a rooting mixture; aluminum foil is used to support the leaf. From *African Violets: Gifts from Nature*

Question 191 **My leaf cuttings take longer to develop new plants than they should. After the roots formed I set the stem, with its roots, about one inch deep into a rooting mixture and have constantly watched the moisture so the roots and stems did not dry out. Any idea what my problem may be?**

Frequently a rooted leaf cutting is just plain stubborn and takes its time in producing any new shoot growth. This may be the case so you must be patient. However, your plantlets are slow developers for a good reason. You have placed the roots and stem too deep into the rooting mixture, thus causing the plantlets to take much longer to emerge through the inch of rooting mixture. In the future, just barely cover the end of the stem with its roots and the results should be faster developing plantlets.

Question 192 **How is the best way to increase my collection of miniature African violets?**

Leaf propagation is a fast and easy way to add to your collection. Remove the leaf from the third or fourth row of a mature plant and place it in a potting mixture. In a few short weeks the roots and plantlets will begin to grow. Move the new plantlets into individual 2½ inch diameter pots when there are six to eight well developed leaves. Also consider ordering the newest varieties from the *African Violet Magazine*.

Question 193 **Does it matter whether cuttings are rooted in water or in a rooting mixture of some sort?**

I am sure if you ask thirty African violet enthusiasts you will get ten that say root them only in water, ten who prefer using a rooting mixture, and the remaining ten will tell you to use either technique. And in fact, all thirty would be correct. You must experiment with each technique for starting your new plants and decide for yourself which one is best for you and your African violets.

Question 194 **How long should the stem be when rooting cuttings?**

In most cases leave approximately 1½ to 2 inches of stem for the best results. Miniature African violets often do not have a stem this long so when working with these tiny plants leave the stem as long as possible.

Question 195 **Why shouldn't the stem of a cutting touch the side of the container I am using?**

Petiole (stem) rot will kill the leaf. Salts or any injury to the stem, which weakens the plant tissue, will allow rot to develop. Avoid this problem by using plastic toothpicks to prop up the leaves, holding them clear of the sides of the container in which you are rooting the leaf.

Do not use wooden toothpicks. Water will be absorbed by the wooden toothpicks and move up the wood. This will encourage petiole (stem) rot where the toothpicks touch the petiole.

Question 196 **After the cutting has sent up several plants how big should these new plants be before moving them into pots?**

I usually wait until the new plants are 1 to 1½ inches tall before moving them into individual pots. The best time to separate all the plants into individual ones and pot them separately is when you remove them from the rooting medium. Pots should be 2 to 2½ inches in diameter and the new plants will remain in these pots for several months.

CREATING NEW PLANTS

Question 197 **I would like to try my hand at creating some new African violets. Where can I find information on this subject?**

Go to your local library and tell them you are looking for a horticulture book that will explain basic genetics and hybridization techniques. Check with your African violet friends. If they have a copy of *African Violets: Gifts from Nature* there is a chapter in it providing basic plant genetic information. Dr. Jeff Smith, a professor at Ball State University in Indiana, writes an excellent column on hybridizing African violets for the *African Violet Magazine*. If you have access to this magazine the information in his articles will be invaluable to you.

Question 198 **What are the yellow things in the center of the flower?**

Those yellow structures you are referring to are the male part of the flower and are called anthers. This is where the pollen (male germ cells) is formed in all flowering plants.

Question 199 **I would like to know if there is a particular time of the year which is best for pollinating African violets and cross-breeding them?**

The best time is in the late spring and during the warm summer days when there is plenty of sunshine. Both these conditions (heat and sunshine) will promote good, healthy African violets which are capable of developing mature, viable seed. If the plants are actively growing it will take a shorter period of time for the seed to mature.

African Violets Back to the Basics

When your plants are being grown under lights you can proceed with your hybridization program anytime of the year. Plants whose flowers are pollinated in the spring will produce good, viable seed in three to six months. The same plants may take up to nine months for seed development if the flowers are pollinated in the fall.

Question 200 **What are some of the dominant and recessive traits commonly seen in African violets?**

The dominant color of the African violet blossoms is blue. It will mask the white, pink, red, and other colors often seen in the flowers. Red will be the dominant trait when crossing plants with pink, and white blossoms. The genes control leaf shape also. Plain or tailored leaves are always a dominant trait as is the all green leaves over variegated leaves.

Remember for a plant to show a recessive trait both of the genes on the pair of matched chromosomes must be recessive. For a dominant trait to develop only one of the two genes must show dominance.

Dr. Jeff Smith developed the following table for his column, written for the *African Violet Magazine,* characterizing how the inheritance of flower color is genetically controlled. He states, "…some colors are intermediate and cannot be listed as a simple dominant or recessive. In these cases, the color can be both depending on what they are compared to. This table (developed by Dr. Smith) will help to clarify these instances."

Inheritance Of Flower Color

Dominant Colors [and corresponding]	Recessive Colors
blue	all other flower colors
red	pink, white
geneva edges	solid edges
all colors	white
non-coral colors	coral colors
raspberry edges	solid edges
pale colors	dark colors
fantasy pattern	solid pattern

Question 201 **Is it very difficult to cross different African violets and obtain new varieties?**

The process of actual crossing two plants is not a difficult task. Simply remove the stamens from one plant, slice through the anthers (yellow structures in center of the flower) and brush the dissected anthers against the stigma (female part of the flower; thin, thread-like structure in the center of the flower) of another African violet. Now all you have to do is sit back and wait several months until the new seeds are matured.

Melvin J. Robey

    Once you have the seed the task starts to become a little more complicated. When all the seeds germinate and the plants start to grow you must be prepared to eliminate all those plans, which do not display any new traits. If you do not do this and you continue cross breedig, you will end up with a house full of Africn violets and very litle room let foryo

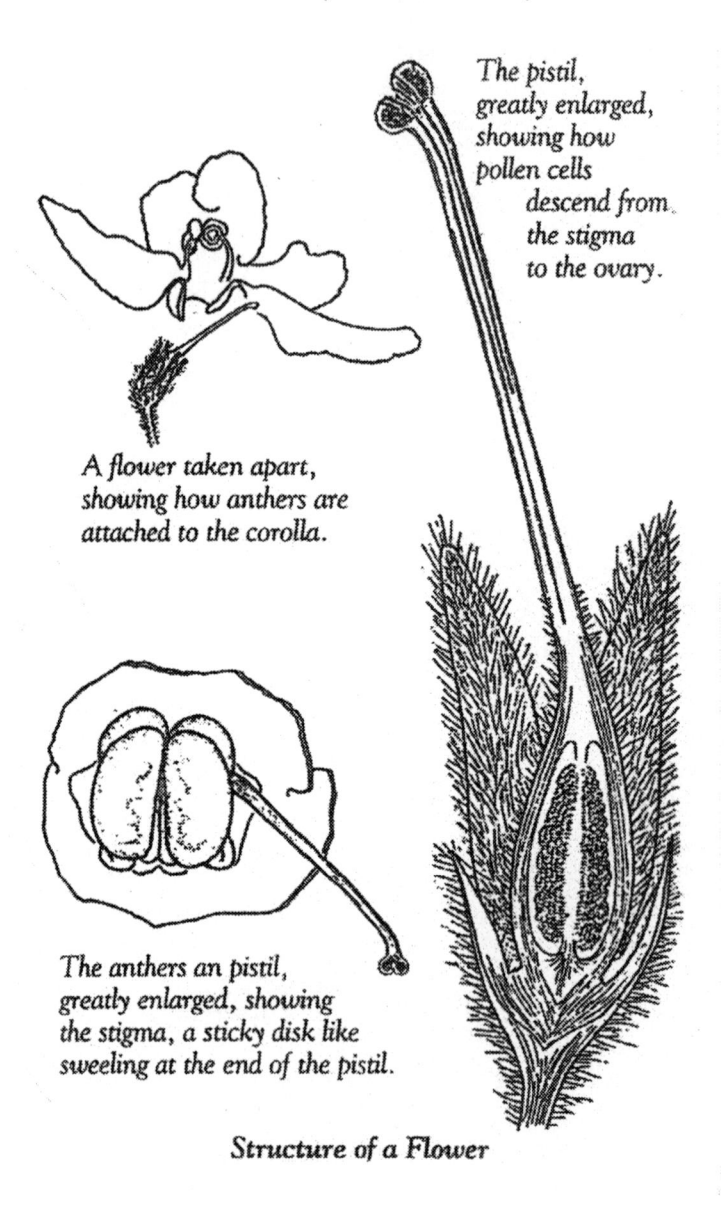

The pistil, greatly enlarged, showing how pollen cells descend from the stigma to the ovary.

A flower taken apart, showing how anthers are attached to the corolla.

The anthers an pistil, greatly enlarged, showing the stigma, a sticky disk like sweeling at the end of the pistil.

Structure of a Flower

Courtesy of the African Violet Society of America

Question 202 **Can I mail pollen from an unusual African violet to another grower who wants to cross one of her plants with mine? And if it is okay to mail pollen how do I protect it so it is still alive when it gets there?**

You can mail the pollen from your plant anywhere without having to worry about its condition upon arrival at its destination. All you have to do is collect the pollen and air-dry it first, then seal it in a small paper envelope and put it in the mail. If you use a plastic bag chances are mildew will form on the seeds, reducing the chances the seed will remain viable. This is especially true if any moisture is present in the bag.

Question 203 **After I have pollinated a flower, how long will it take before I have mature seeds ready for planting?**

The actual length of time will vary depending on which African violets you are working with. A miniature plant will produce mature seed in three to four months, while the larger Supremes may take up to six months. Watch the seedpod to determine when the seeds are ready for removal. The pod will become wrinkled and brown when the seeds are mature. When this happens the seeds are not yet ready to be planted. After the pods have been removed they should be kept in a small envelope and placed in a warm spot to allow the seeds to dry. Be sure to label the envelope so you know which plant the pod came from. The seed will be ready for planting after four weeks of this drying process.

Question 204 **When the seedpod matures, how many seed can I expect to obtain from the pod?**

This will vary from plant to plant but usually four to six hundred seeds per pod is considered good.

Question 205 **Can you give me some tips on growing new plants from seeds?**

The African violet seeds are very small, sometimes characterized as being "dust-like." Sprinkle the seeds onto a moist rooting medium that has been sterilized. Germinating seeds are extremely susceptible to a disease called "damping off." *Pythium* and *Rhizoctonia* are the two fungi that attack the small plants as they emerge from the seeds. Sterilization will stop these pests from causing you a problem. The seeds should not be buried in the rooting mixture but left on the surface. Covering the seeds with a clear plastic will help hold the moisture around them and speed up germination. Do not forget to give the seeds strong light while waiting for the new plants to develop. After sowing the tiny seeds you can expect 70 to 90 percent of the them to germinate by the end of 21 days. However, a few may germinate as quickly as in 7 days.

Question 206 **I would like to do some cross breeding between variegated African violets and some plants with all green leaves. Are the two types of plants receptive to being cross pollinated?**

All African violets can be cross-pollinated with one another since they are in the same genus. Certain varieties are much easier to work with than others. You will not have any trouble in your hybridization (breeding) program using variegated plants unless you want the new plants developing from the seed to have variegated leaves. If this is your goal you must follow one simple rule to be successful.

<u>Rule</u>

The variegated plant must always be the seed plant. By this I mean you must transfer the pollen from the all green leaf plant to the variegated plant's stigma.

Question 207 **What is colchicine? I once heard it was a chemical that could be used in creating new varieties. Is this correct?**

The answer to your second question is, yes. This powerful chemical may be used in the search for newer, better varieties of African violets. Colchicine is a toxic chemical and should be handled carefully. I would not recommend anyone use this chemical, other than a trained scientist.

When a plant is treated with this chemical the walls between the individual plant cells are dissolved, causing the chromosome number to double in each of the newly formed cells. These plants are often referred to as polyploids—having an extra set (sometimes more) of chromosomes in each cell. This often results in plants with thicker, bigger leaves, and larger blossoms. Supreme, DuPont, and Amazon varieties of African violets are usually formed by using colchicines.

CHAPTER 9

THE ENVIRONMENT AROUND YOUR PLANTS

TEMPERATURE CONTROLS ESSENTIAL

Question 208 **The name—African violet—suggests this plant needs to be kept in a warm place to do well. Is this true?**
You will probably be surprised at how cool the temperature can be while the African violet is producing beautiful blossoms. African violets prefer a temperature between 70 to 75 degrees Fahrenheit but will tolerate temperatures as low as 55 to 60 degrees. Try to keep your plants in a spot in your home where the day and night time temperatures do not vary more than five to eight degrees. Large temperature fluctuations are not good for an African violet.

Question 209 **Does the room temperature have anything to do with the flowering of African violets?**
Yes. If you allow the temperature to drop down into the low fifties your plants will get chilled and refuse to produce any flowers. At these lower temperatures the plants will survive and remain healthy. If you have to have temperatures this low in your home select variegated African violets. Without flowers these plants are still pleasing to the eye and will occasionally flower for you.
Anytime you have plants in a location where the temperature fluctuates widely, say from 85 degrees Fahrenheit in the daytime to 60 degrees Fahrenheit at night, chances are your African violets will stop flowering for you.

Melvin J. Robey

A thermometer among the plants on a light stand allows the author to easily monitor the temperature. (MJR)

From *African Violets: Gifts from Nature*

***Question 210** Besides turning up the thermostat, how else can the temperature be kept higher to help seeds germinate?*

There is a simple technique you can use. Place a cover over the container in which the seeds are planted. A clear plastic tent can be used to form a miniature greenhouse over the seeds. Provide some air movement around the seeds and do not let the humidity get to high. When water collects on the cover take a cloth and wipe it off. It is also important the cover allows the light through to the seeds. A 40 to 60-watt incandescent light bulb can also be placed near the seed. The bulb will generate heat and help to warm up the potting mixture. There are some commercially made seed boxes with warming cables along the bottom of the box. The heating cable acts like an electric blanket, keeping the potting mixture warm for excellent seed germination.

***Question 211** Is there any difference between the temperature requirements for getting seed to germinate and growing mature plants?*

Yes. There is a slight difference between the temperature requirements. The mature plant does not need to be as warm as is needed to get the seeds to germinate. With germinating seeds you need to try to keep the temperature warmer, around 75 to 85 degrees Fahrenheit and you will see some of the seeds come to life in about two weeks. However, it can take as long as eight to ten weeks for all the seeds to germinate.

Question 212 Why does the temperature have to be higher for seed germination?

The moist potting mixture in which the seeds are laying tends to be cool. It takes a higher temperature to warm up the mixture to a point where the seeds will germinate. A cold mixture will slow down the germination process and can even cause the seeds to refuse to germinate. In extreme cases the seeds will absorb the water but instead of germinating they will rot. For a higher percent of seed germination keep the temperature higher than normal.

Question 213 During the cool fall nights I worry about my plants setting on the windowsills. How can I protect them from the cold nights without moving them out of the window every night? Later, I will move them from the windows for the winter months but I hate to do this early in the fall.

Your problem is an easy one to solve. Take some cardboard boxes and cut up pieces you can slip between the window and your plants. Cardboard is an excellent insulating material and will protect the plants from the cool weather. There is a limit to how well this technique works so do not wait too late into the fall before moving your plants out of the windows. Be sure the leaves do not touch the glass or some damage may occur to them.

Question 214 How come some of the leaf tips on my African violets are turning brown and dying? When the temperature starts to cool off in the afternoon I remove the plants from the windowsills.

It may be the leaves are touching the glass and you are not removing the plants from the window early enough. Glass is an excellent conductor of cold and hot temperatures. Even though the air temperatures may be warm the glass cools quickly. If the leaves are touching the window the delicate plant cells may be killed. Be a little more careful with your plants. Do not let the leaves touch the glass. This also is true for the summer months. Heat will kill the cells even quicker than cold does.

Question 215 Up until a few days ago my African violet was absolutely fantastic, producing beautiful bright red blossoms. Then I moved it into the kitchen window by the back door so I could enjoy it more on these cold winter days. All of a sudden it started to droop and the flowers turned brown. What did I do wrong?

A friend on mine called me and told a story almost identical to your question. My suggestion to her was to move the African violet away from the door and to a warmer spot. She did and in a few days the plant was on its way to a full recovery. African violets are extremely sensitive to cold drafts and I suspect every time someone goes in or out your door a cold blast of winter air encompasses the plant. Her plant was not as far gone as yours sounds but go ahead, move your plant away from the door. It may recover and again produce lovely red blossoms for you.

AFRICAN VIOLETS LIKE HUMIDITY

Question 216   What is the ideal humidity for growing African violets in my home?

Ideally, 70 to 80 percent relative humidity would be perfect for these plants. This is the condition found in their native habitat—Africa—where they are found growing in tropical valleys. In the home if you could keep the humidity near 40 percent the plants would be happy. When it is lower than this the plants have a tendency to produce fewer blossoms.

Question 217   I have just moved from Florida to the Chicago area and have noticed the air is much drier here. Is this a normal winter condition for Chicago?

Yes, the air is drier in Chicago than in Florida during the cooler winter months. I am sure the Florida humidity is less in the winter when compared to the summer months. Cold air cannot hold as much moisture as warmer air, causing the drop in the level of moisture found in the air.

Question 218   It is difficult for me to get the humidity high enough in my home to meet the needs of my African violets. Do you have any suggestions on how to solve this problem?

Fortunately you do not have to worry about the humidity of the entire house but only the immediate area around your plants. An easy way to raise the humidity around the plants is to fill up small trays with water and place them among your African violets. The evaporating water will help satisfy the humidity requirements of your plants. If you have any vermiculite, pumice, pebbles, or peat put these materials in a tray of water. This will help hold the moisture longer, releasing it at a more uniform rate.

Question 219   If the humidity is too low what effect will this have on the plant and its ability to produce blossoms?

Your plant will continue to develop a few blossoms but the total number produced will be considerably less. You should be aware the African violet's foliage will suffer too. It will lose its vigor and development of any new leaves is slowed down. Very seldom will too low of humidity cause the death of a plant but its ability to flower may not be up to your expectations.

Question 220 **Which rooms in a home naturally have the highest humidity?**

Probably the highest humidity in your home is near the kitchen sink. Whenever you turn the water on some of it evaporates into the air. Placing your African violets on a windowsill over the sink should produce lovely plants, providing they have plenty of light. Another spot in your home where the humidity will be slightly higher is in the bathrooms, but the lighting is usually not sufficient for healthy plant growth.

Question 221 **Will it hurt my African violets to spray water on them?**

Misting the plants is a good way to satisfy their humidity requirements. This is very beneficial for the plants providing the water is not too cold. Also, do not spray so much water on the plants that it runs down onto the crowns. If this happens crown rot may develop which will eventually kill the plants.

Question 222 **When misting my African violets are there any special problems which I should be aware?**

One consideration was discussed in the preceding question. Two other situations you should avoid when misting African violets are: (1) Do not let them set in a draft when they are wet—a chilled plant will not flower for you. (2) Do not let direct sunlight shine on the wet foliage as this may allow the plants to get leaf burn.

Question 223 **Why is fresh air around the plants so important to their health?**

Fresh air creates an ideal environment for the growth of the plants and enables them to flower profusely. Stale air around the plants increases the chances of disease organisms infecting the plants, wrecking their appearance and often killing them. Another facet of a plant's needs, not completely understood by most gardeners, is the requirement for a continual supply of carbon dioxide. This gas is absorbed by the leaves and is an integral component of the photosynthetic process (production of food which enables the plant to grow and flower). A continual supply of fresh air keeps the carbon dioxide levels high around the plant and this promotes healthy growth with abundant flowering as the end result.

Melvin J. Robey

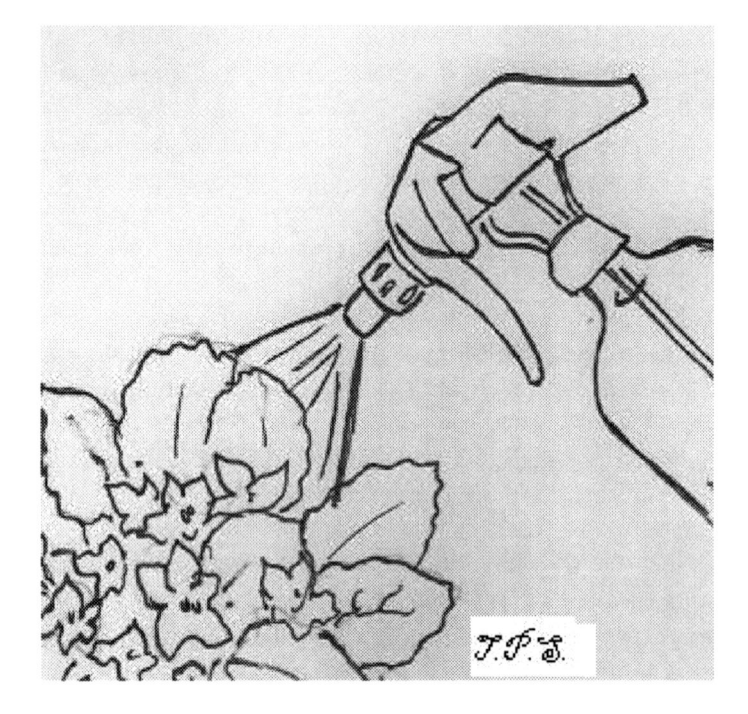

Misting leaves is an excellent technique for increasing humidity around an African violet.

AIR MOVEMENT

Respiration

$$6O_2\uparrow + C_6H_{12}O_6 \rightarrow 6CO_2\uparrow + 6H_2O$$
$$\text{oxygen} \quad \text{sugar} \quad \quad \text{carbon dioxide} \quad \text{water}$$

$\uparrow$ indicates a compound is a gas

$\rightarrow$ shows two compounds on the left are converted to the compounds on the right

Question 224 A lot of the material I read places considerable emphasis on allowing good air movement into the potting mixture. If the plant satisfies its air requirements around its leaves why does it need air in the potting mixture?

This is a simple question to answer and it is a complex process known as respiration. Scientists have been studying it for years. The plant's leaves remove carbon dioxide from the air for photosynthesis, while the plant's roots are absorbing oxygen from the air in the potting mixture.

Respiration occurs 24 hours a day in every cell in a plant, converting sugars to energy for the plants continual growth. The roots and leaves use the oxygen in several important growing processes and release carbon dioxide back into the atmosphere.

ature 225 When growing African violets what is the most common mistake made by the beginner?

After a person falls into the "African Violet Trap" the trended is often to go out and buy as many of these lovely plants as the budget or room in the home will allow. What happens next is the crowding together of plants because of inadequate space for all of them. This creates numerous problems for the plants: a lack of adequate sunlight, reduction of air movement among the plants, excellent conditions for disease and insect problems to develop, and difficulty to water all the plants properly.

It is best to avoid overcrowded conditions. When buying plants there is a tendency to forget that in a few short months their size will increase, leading to overcrowding of the plants. If the leaves of the plants are touching then you need to move some of the plants to another spot.

Question 226 **Basements are always stuffy and I was wondering if I needed to use a fan to stir up the air around my African violets? I have approximately 300 plants growing under lights in my basement.**

Anytime you have a large number of African violets growing under lights there is a good chance overcrowded conditions exist. This will lead to stale air, allowing disease problems to develop. Your idea of using a fan to circulate air among your plants is a good one so long as you observe a few simple rules.

Never aim the fan directly at the plants. Direct the airflow about twelve to eighteen inches above them. This will create the desired air circulation around the plants. Always avoid blowing extremely cold air onto or around the plants. Set the fan so it is drawing room temperature air and not a blast of cold air that is continually tumbling down the stairs. A fan with a twelve-inch diameter will do the job for you. Set it on its slowest speed.

Question 227 **Of the African violet diseases, which one is most likely to occur when there is poor air movement around the plants?**

Botrytis Gray Mold is the culprit you will encounter first. This disease thrives when the air is stale, the humidity high, and when the leaves and blossoms remain wet too long. Another disease to show up under these conditions is powdery mildew.

Question 228 **If air movement around the plants is important, how come miniature African violets do okay enclosed in terrariums?**
The reason African violets can be grown successfully in terrariums is the special attention given to them in this type situation. If you try growing them in a terrarium and do not pay attention to what you are doing the temperature becomes to high and it becomes very humid. When this happens the air becomes stale, the leaves have water on them, and Botrytis Gray Mold will attack the plants. Keeping an eye on the terrarium allows you to remove the lid when you see moisture accumulating on the glass. By doing this you let in fresh air, while the water-laden air escapes from the terrarium.

Question 229 **My African violets set on the windowsills in my home. Would it be okay to open the windows and let the fresh air flow around my plants?**
The outside air temperature will determine if you can open the windows near your plants. Remember a cool draft on the plants will make them sick, often severely damaging them or even killing them. Check the air temperature, if it is warmer than 75 degrees Fahrenheit your plants will not be damaged. Do not forget that as the sun sets the temperature drops, so close the windows early in the afternoon.

Another important consideration is, do your windows have screens on them and what is the size of the openings in the screen? A lack of screens will allow many different types of insects into the home and many of them are small enough to crawl through the tiniest of openings in window screens.

Question 230 **On one of my variegated plants the flowers dropped off shortly after they opened. The flowers still look healthy and pretty when this happened so a disease must not be the cause. What is my problem?**
Check the air temperature in the room. If you are circulating too hot of air then this probably is causing your problem. Low humidity combined with the hot air will aid in the premature dropping of the healthy flowers.

Temperature Comparisons

Celsius	Fahrenheit
0	32
10	50
20	68
30	86
40	104

CHAPTER 10

LIGHT AND ITS ROLE IN A PLANT'S LIFE

Question 231 **Can you give me an explanation of how the sunlight is converted into energy a plant can utilize?**

The sunlight is not converted into energy but is the driving force which causes the energy to be manufactured in the leaves. As the light strikes the plants the individual wavelengths (red and blue) are absorbed by the leaves. Inside the leaves the chloroplasts have structures in them specifically designed to absorb these sun rays. Chloroplasts are able to convert light energy into a usable form (sugar) for the plant's growing processes. This entire process is known as photosynthesis.

PHOTOSYNTHESIS CHEMICAL EQUATION

$$6CO_2\uparrow + 6H_2O + \text{sunlight} \rightarrow C_6H_{12}O_6 + 6O_2\uparrow + H_2O$$

carbon dioxide   water   sugar   oxygen   water

$\uparrow$ indicates a compound is a gas

$\rightarrow$ shows two compounds on the left are converted to the compounds on the right

Question 232 **Can you a give me a simple answer to what the difference is between photosynthesis and respiration in a plant?**

The simplest way to explain these two physiological processes is: photosynthesis manufactures the food (sugar) plants need for their development and respiration uses the food (sugar) as an energy source to carry out various functions throughout the plants.

Question 233 *Just how much light do my African violets require for healthy growth and to produce numerous blossoms?*

African violets should receive at least 400 to 600 foot candles of light if they are to develop the flowers you are anticipating. Place the plants where brightness of the light is in the 800 to 1,100 foot candle range and the results will be even more spectacular. The plants will produce approximately thirty percent more flowers at this higher light intensity.

For the best results, at any light intensity, the African violets should be exposed to the light for ten to sixteen hours a day. It is important to the plants well being that they are immersed in total darkness for at least eight hours every day.

<u>Definition of foot candles</u>

Foot candle is a term used to measure the brightness of the light reaching the plants; scientifically, it is defined as the amount of light one candle radiates on an object one foot from the flame; abbreviated f.c. The easiest way to check the foot candles of light reaching your plants is to use a light meter designed for photography.

Question 234 *My plants are in a west window where the sun shines directly on them. Is this good or bad for the plants?*

African violets are able to withstand two to three hours of direct sun in the spring, winter, and fall. During these times of the year the sunlight's intensity is reduced and is very beneficial to the plants. In the summer when the sun is higher in the sky the direct sun rays on the plants can be harmful. Move the plants to a north window or farther back into the room from your west window and they will be okay in the summer.

Question 235 *Often my friends disagree on which window location is best for growing African violets. I have become confused after listening to them and was wondering if you could help me out?*

When discussing window locations for growing African violets there are a lot of factors which have to be considered. Some of these are: time of the year, time of the day sun enters the windows, how far the plants are from the windows, are the windows draped, are the windows shaded by trees, and the type of African violet—all must be considered. Another important factor is where you live—how far north or south your home is located.

African Violets Back to the Basics

In the summertime a north window is an excellent choice but in the winter the plants will have to be relocated because of insufficient light coming through the windows. Generally, for year round use, east and west windows are ideally suited if the light is filtering through trees or drapes to help cut down on the light's intensity. This is especially true in the summer months. South windows are best in the wintertime when the sun is not as strong and the plants can set in full sunshine for a few hours each day without becoming sun scorched.

Question 236 **How bright is the light, which comes through the various windows in my house during the winter months?**

The sunlight's intensity shining through the different windows in your home will vary depending on the time of day, cloud cover, other atmospheric conditions, and where you live.

During the brightest time of the day measurements of up to 5,000 foot-candles have been recorded for windows located on the south side of a home. East and west windows average somewhere between 250 and 500 foot candles, while north windows let in 125 to 250 foot candles of light at noon. Let a cloud cover move into the sky and the light intensity is greatly reduced.

Question 237 **Why are the stems of my African violet leaves always bending towards the light? I have noticed this happens all the time and it is ruining the appearance of my plants.**

Fortunately this is not a permanent condition. Simply start rotating the pots about a quarter turn once a week, allowing the light to strike a new area of the plant.

There is a chemical, called auxin, in the stems of the plants and it is very sensitive to light. When the light shines on the stems this chemical moves to the opposite side of the stem, sort of like it was trying to hide from the sun. This causes a build up of the auxin on the side away from the direction from which the light is coming. Another characteristic of auxin is it causes the cells to elongate rapidly when it becomes concentrated on one side of the stems. This causes the cells to grow faster, thus causing the stems to bend towards the light.

Question 238 **I am growing my African violets under fluorescent lights and the leaves are growing straight up—sort of like they were reaching towards the light. What can I do to make these plants grow correctly?**

Melvin J. Robey

The problem is you are not giving the African violets sufficient light. Either add additional light fixtures or move the lights closer to the plants. Use a light meter to check the light's intensity at the tops of the plants. It should be at least 400 to 600 foot candles and can be as high as 1,100 f.c.

Courtesy of Sylvania

Question 239 In an artificial lighting set-up what affects the amount of light reaching the plants below?

There are four basic factors, which affect the lighting of the plants growing below artificial lights.

1. The number of light fixtures you are using; two bulbs produce twice as much light as one.
2. Distance between the lights and the plants; the farther away the fixtures are from the plants, the weaker the light reaching them.
3. Light emitted from the center of a fluorescent tube is stronger than that coming from the ends of the tube. The plants on the outer edges of the light will receive less light than the plants directly under the light fixture.
4. Age of the light fixture governs the amount of light given off to the plants below.

Question 240 **What symptoms do African violets show when they are receiving too much light?**

There are five easily recognizable signs caused by excessive light reaching the African violets.
1. Leaves lose their nice green color, becoming yellowish and sick looking; variegated leaves become all green
2. The mature leaves will bend down over the edge of the pot instead of standing out parallel to the shelf or counter on which the pot is sitting
3. Petioles (stems) of the younger leaves become stubby
4. The center of the plant becomes overcrowded; this compacted growth is not healthy for the African violets
5. Developing flower stalks are stunted and unable to push up through the dense (compacted) leaf growth in the center of the plant

Question 241 **How can I tell if my plants are not getting enough light?**

Using a light meter to measure the brightness of the light works well. There should be a minimum of 400 to 600 foot candles of light for adequate growth of the plants.

The appearance of your African violets will tell you if they are receiving sufficient light. If the plants are only producing a few flowers, the leaves are yellowish-green, and the leaf stems are elongated then you can be certain the lighting is to poor for the development of healthy African violets. Move them to a spot where there is better lighting.

Question 242 **I have been told the length of time I leave my fluorescent lights on has an effect on the development of my African violets. Can you explain to me the effect different lengths of light exposure have on my plants?**

The best way to answer your question is to develop a table so you can conveniently compare the amount of light the plants receive and the effect of the light on their growth and flowering.

Effect of Varying Lengths of Light Periods on the Development of African Violets

Amount of Light Exposure(500 foot candles) in a Day	Plant Development
Less than 12 hours	A new leaf will form every 7-14 days. A flowering potential is built up during this time and a few flowers will eventually develop.
12 to 14 hours	New leaves will form every 5 to 7 days; a new flower stalk will emerge every 5 to 7 days.
14 to 16 hour	The new leaves form quickly; their growth is stunted, causing the center of the plant to become compacted. Emerging flower stalks are also stunted and cannot push up through the compacted leaves in the center of the plant.
More than 16 hours	Leaves become yellowish, stunted, and the center of the plant is a mass of tightly form leaves. The leaves may become scorched

Question 243 **What is the difference between a Gro-Lux and a fluorescent light fixture?**

Both types of light fixtures produce good light for growing African violets. They emit a high percentage of their light in the red and blue wavelengths, which the plants need for healthy growth. The Gro-Lux has a better balance of the red and blue rays than does a fluorescent light fixture. Because of this and the greater amount of red rays produced, the Gro-Lux radiates a pinkish or rose colored light. The importance of this balanced lighting is readily spotted because it usually increases the number of buds and flowers by approximately fifty percent.

Question 244 **Does the age of a fluorescent light have any connection with the flowering of African violets?**

It certainly does. As a light fixture gets older it is less effective in producing light for your plants. This means the light fixture is producing less light after six months of use. An African violet can easily sense this change in light quantity and will produce fewer and fewer flowers as the fluorescent light gets weaker and weaker from continuous use.

Question 245 **I've noticed a gray ring around both ends of my fluorescent tubes. What is causing this?**

Old age is the problem. You have been using the tubes for a long time and this smoke ring is an indication they have been around for a while. You should keep a record of when you put new fluorescent tubes in the fixture and replace them at least once year.

Question 246 **There are so many different types of light fixtures I don't know which ones to use. Can you help me?**

Basically, your choices are limited to three distinct categories: incandescent, fluorescent, and agricultural lamps.

<u>Incandescent Bulbs</u>

Ordinary light bulbs used in lamps around your home are incandescent bulbs. For plants these bulbs produce a light which is rich in the red color and that is ideal for causing African violets to flower. The problem with these bulbs is they give off a tremendous amount of heat and can very easily damage your favorite plants. For this reason they are not used too often in artificial light setups.

<u>Fluorescent Tubes</u>

These lamps are an excellent source of a well balance light for African violets. The light produced is good for promoting both the growth of the plant and the formation of flower buds. Usually two-48 inch long (40 watts each) tubes are used for lighting. These fixtures produce very little heat, which makes them ideally suited for use.

<u>Agriculture Lamps</u>

You will recognize these lights anytime you see them because of the rose to purplish glow they emit. Excellent results have been obtained by growing African violets under these lights. Gro-Lux is just one brand name available when you go to the garden center to buy them.

Question 247 **Why aren't African violets grown under regular light bulbs?**

The regular light bulbs—incandescent bulbs—emit light that encourages flowering in the plant but does very little for the development of healthy leaves. Another reason is the incandescent bulbs give off too much heat and can damage the plants if the user is not extremely careful.

Question 248   Why not grow African violets under artificial lights twenty-four hours a day if they do so well when they receive lots of light?

A plant always maintains a delicate balance within itself, which controls how well it performs. When you upset the internal physiological functions (biological clock) of a plant, by giving it too much or to little of something, the plant will respond abnormally. This is what will happen if you give your plants continuous light for any length of time. During the dark period the plant continues to produce chemicals which react with those manufactured in the light, releasing a combination of ingredients which cause the plant to produce beautiful leaves and fantastic blossoms.

Question 249   Do I have to give my African violets special care when they are being grown under the lights?

Yes, since you are giving the plants the best possible light for rapid growth and maximum flowering you should pay extra attention to feeding them, watering them, and keeping a close watch on the air temperature. Because your plants are actively growing they will need extra food and more water to meet their needs. Try to maintain the temperatures somewhere in the neighborhood of 70 to 75 degrees F. for the healthiest plants.

Question 250   At what distance should the fluorescent lights be set above the plants?

Normally the distance can be set at eighteen inches from the top of the plants to the fluorescent tubes. If you have young plants just getting started you can lower the lights six inches. Remember as the days turn into weeks these plants will be continuously growing. Therefore every once in a while it will be necessary for you to raise the lights to allow for the new growth of the plants.

GLOSSARY

Acid: Any substance with a pH less than 7.0; any compound which releases hydrogen (H⁺) ions in a chemical reaction in the potting mixture or water solution.

Alkaline: Any substance with a pH greater than 7.0; any compound, which releases hydroxyl (OH⁻) ions in a chemical reaction in the potting mixture or water solution.

Amazon: Plants with larger than normal leaves and flowers; tetraploid chromosome count causes increase in size.

Anthers: Yellow saclike structures extending from the center of the flower; one of two structures, which make up the stamens; the male or pollen grains (gametes) are contained in the anthers.

Auxin: A naturally occurring hormone found in plants; may also be synthetically produced in laboratories; promotes cell elongation and enlargement.

Bicolored blossoms: Blossoms displaying two distinct colors in the petals.

Carrier: An inert material mixed with the fertilizer nutrients; useful in allowing the fertilizer nutrients to be uniformly distributed throughout the fertilizers product.

Chimera(chimaera): A mixture of cells, of diverse genetic information; African violets with pinwheel blossoms are often a result of this condition.

Chromosome: Microscopic, rod-like structure composed of individual units (genes) which pass a plant's characteristics from generation to generation.

Crown: Portion of an African violet plant located just above the potting mixture surface; new leaves and flower stalks originate from the crown.

Crown rot: A disease which attacks the crown of the plant; usually resulting in the death of the plant.

Cultivar: Plant developed by man through hybridization or by a mutation occurring in a collection plants.

Disbudding: Removal of the flower buds before they open.

Division: The cutting apart of a plant having two or more crowns with a single mass of commonly shared roots.

DuPont: *See* Amazon.

Fertilizer grade: The percentage of nitrogen, phosphorus, and potassium contained in a fertilize product; ie. 5-0-7.

Footcandle: A term used to measure the brightness of the light reaching the plants; scientifically, it is defined as the amount of light one candle radiates on an object one foot from the flame; abbreviated f.c.

Gamete: A male (pollen) or female (ovule) reproductive cell, containing one-half (haploid) of the chromosomes needed for fertilization and seed formation.

Genus; genera (pl.): A grouping of plants with similar characteristics differing markedly from other groups of plants; first word in the scientific name of a plant; i.e. *Saintpaulia*.

Hybrid: A plant developed by cross-pollinating two different plants, usually producing offspring with new characteristics.

Leach: Movement of water down through a potting mixture, dissolving plant nutrients and other chemicals (salts), washing them out the bottom of pots with drain holes.

Leaf margin: Outer most edge of a leaf.

Macronutrients: Six major plant food nutrients (nitrogen, phosphorus, potassium, calcium, magnesium, and sulfur) needed in large quantities by plants for normal growth and development.

Micronutrients: Seven essential plant food nutrients (boron, chlorine, iron, manganese, molybdenum, copper, and zinc) needed in only small quantities by plants.

Minor nutrients: *See* Micronutrients.

Multicolored blossoms: Any blossom which displays two or more colors in the petals.

Mutant: See sport.

Necky plant: A plant which has lost several leaves from the lower whorls of leaves, exposing the main stalk above the potting mixture.

pH: Scientific measurement used to determine if the potting mixture or any other substance is acid, alkaline, or neural; a pH number below 7.0 is acid, above 7.0 is alkaline, and a pH of 7.0 is neutral.

Photosynthesis: The production of food (sugar and starch) in plants through a complex chemical reaction involving light, water, and carbon dioxide; only occurs in green plants.

Plantlet: A young plant, which is developing from a leaf cutting.

Resting period: The period of time between when an African violet stops flowering and then starts flowering again.

Respiration: The process in which plants convert stored food (sugar & starch) into energy for growth and flower development.

Rosette (of leaves): A circular arrangement of the leaves, formed as they radiate out in all directions over the edge of the pot.

Separation: The process of separating two or more intertwined plants, each with its own root system.

Side shoot: See sucker.

Soil ball: Roots and potting mixture mass formed when plants are grown in pots and containers.

Somatic tissue: Plant tissue having paired chromosomes, one chromosome set from each of the parent plants; referred to as vegetative growth.

Species: A group of plants very closely related which display similar characteristics; a unit of plant classification; second word in the scientific name of a plant; i.e. *ionantha*.

Sport: Any plant displaying a marked variation from the parent plant; deviation in appearance may occur in the leaves or flowers or both; also referred to as a mutant.

Suckers: Side shoots that develop from the leaf axil or base of the crown; if allowed to grow, a multiple crowned plant will develop.

Supreme: *See* Amazon.

Tepid water: Moderately warm water; lukewarm.

Tetraploid: Plants whose cells contain twice the normal diploid number of chromosomes; four complete sets of chromosomes; designated 4n; Amazon, DuPont, and Supreme African violets are tetraploid.

Trace nutrients: *See* Micronutrients.

Variegated leaf: Refers to plant foliage, which shows a combination of two different colors; green with splotches of white on the leaf is the most common.

ABOUT THE AUTHOR

The author's first book, *African Violets: Queens of the Indoor Gardening Kingdom*, was hailed as a tribute to the Queen of the indoor gardening kingdom. Enthusiastic African violet fans have referred to his second book, *African Violets: Gifts from Nature*, as a "Masterpiece" and as "a must have for your African violet library." Mr. Robey continues his reign as the African Queen's devoted King with the publication of his third book on America's most popular flowering houseplant—and promises it is not his last.

Mel Robey uses his unique knowledge of the plant world to explain to the reader the basic skills required to produce beautiful African violets. His down-to-earth, easy-to-understand approach to writing is the key to his success as an author.

The author is also a well known agronomic expert in the sports world. Through his lifelong efforts and those of many others at Purdue University, numerous professional and college sports fields converted from artificial turf to a natural grass playing field. The most notable was when the San Francisco 49'ers and Giants decide to be the first to tear out the Astroturf in Candlestick Park, replacing it with one of Mr. Robey's patented designs.

Mr. Robey has a Bachelor of Science degree from Utah State University and a Master's degree from Purdue University. Both degrees specialized in botany, horticulture, and agronomy.

Mr. Robey divides his time between living in southern California's desert area near Palm Springs and Pattaya/Jomtien, Thailand. Besides writing, his other hobbies include: golfing, fishing, and traveling.

Selected Illustrations by Terry Sheehan (T.P.S.)

Mr. Terry Sheehan studied drawing and composition, basic design and color at College of the Desert in Palm Desert, California. Terry began his art career in the second grade; his first floral object was a rose. Flowers and nature drawings are his favorite subjects. In his spare time Mr. Sheehan volunteers as an art instructor at a Boys and Girls Club.